Steam to the Summit

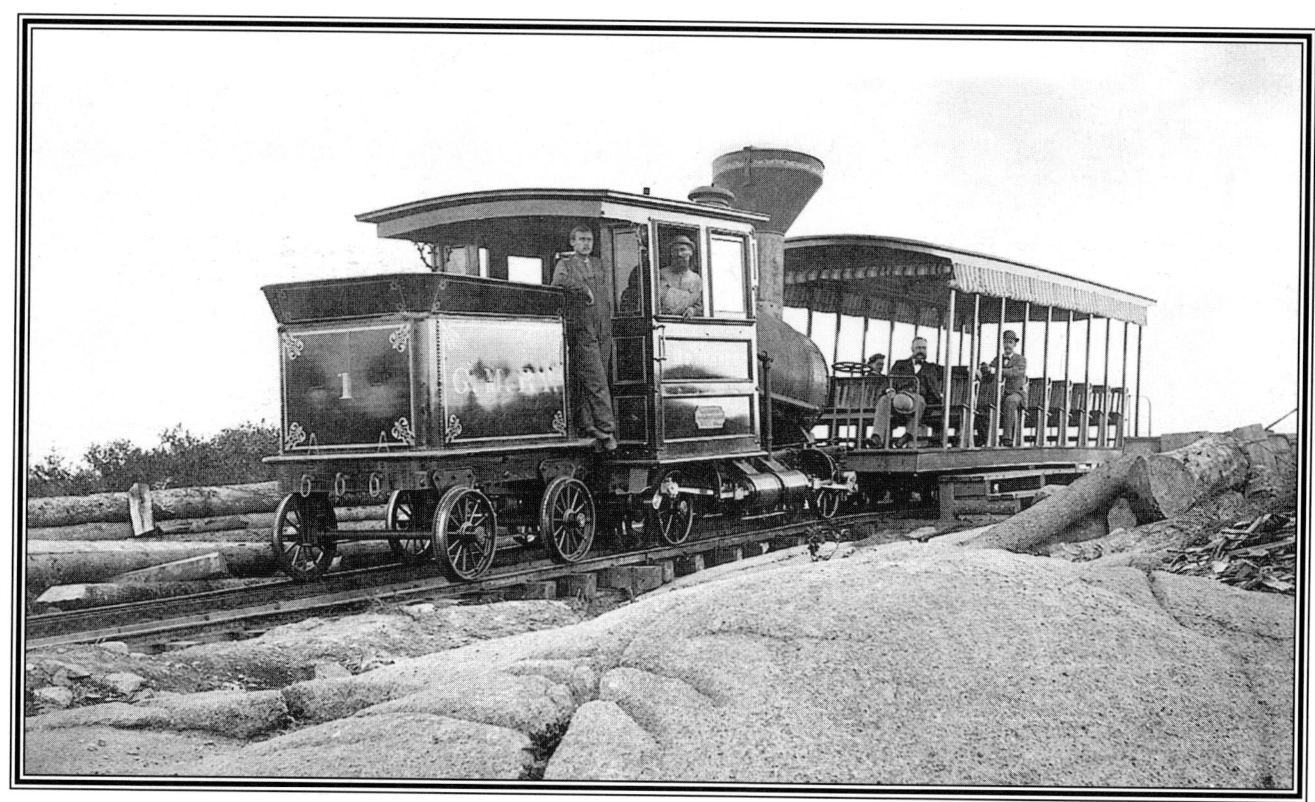

Green Mountain Railway locomotive No. 1 first reached the summit of Green Mountain on June 22, 1883. The sturdy workhorse, also known as *Mount Desert,* was built at the Manchester Locomotive Works, a well-regarded New Hampshire firm that had previously fashioned similar engines for the Mount Washington Railway.

Steam to the Summit

The Green Mountain Railway
Bar Harbor's Remarkable Cog Railroad

PETER DOW BACHELDER

Printed in the United States of America

First Edition

The Breakwater Press
P.O. Box 367
Ellsworth, Maine 04605-0367

Cover and text design by Janet L. Patterson, Rockland, Maine

ISBN 0-9664831-1-1

On the cover:
Green Mountain Railway locomotive *Mount Desert* shortly after its arrival at the foot of Green Mountain—early May 1883.
Courtesy of Mount Desert Island Historical Society

CONTENTS

ACKNOWLEDGMENTS

For many years I'd been aware that a cog railroad once operated on the slopes of today's Cadillac Mountain at Bar Harbor, but it wasn't until the spring of 2001, when I enjoyed an eye-opening trek along its overgrown roadbed, that I became curious enough to want to delve into the details of the story. Why such an unusual venture in the first place? It seemed so out of character with the surroundings. Who attempted it? Was it a success? Whatever became of it? I had lots of questions. What were the answers?

A quick check in nearby libraries turned up little more than cursory mention of what was once called the Green Mountain Railway, so named after Cadillac's previous designation. In local histories I found an occasional picture of the curious little train that chugged up and down the mountain during the latter part of the nineteenth century. Usually they were accompanied by a few sentences about the railroad's relatively brief existence, but that was all. Rather than being disappointed or losing interest, though, I decided to keep looking. I soon came up with a couple of short articles dating from the 1940s and 1950s. These helped, but I still wanted to know more. Before long I was investigating in earnest.

Research is like detective work; both require a great deal of patience and persistence. More often than not, the hunt for specific details leads to dead ends or conflicting information—or both. And that can become extremely frustrating. Research is also difficult, if not impossible to accomplish alone. To be effective it inevitably entails the support and assistance of a network of cooperative, resourceful individuals, each willing and able to lend a helping hand. The challenge is to locate them. In this instance I was more than fortunate to have gained the unfailing help of an extraordinary group of people who, in short, have made the whole project a remarkable learning experience—and a lot of fun.

Randall H. Bennett is the Assistant Director/Curator of Collections at the Bethel Historical Society. He is also an accomplished author/historian and a long-time friend. Randy accompanied me on one of my early explorations along the Green Mountain Railway's old roadbed and shared my early enthusiasm when I resolved to uncover more of the railroad's history. Through the entire course of the work he remained a staunch and loyal advocate. On several occasions he located rare images and ferreted out meaningful details. He likewise steered me through a lean time, when my progress was flagging and the satisfactory completion of the entire undertaking seemed doubtful. His ever-encouraging words were always timely and on more than one occasion lifted my spirits immeasurably.

Will Anderson, a highly talented Maine author and publisher in his own right, has likewise provided noteworthy encouragement and keen insight throughout the project. His willingness to share the storehouse of knowledge he possesses in all phases of the "book business" have been at once enlightening, meaningful, and highly appreciated.

Richard R. Shaw, a gifted historian and writer, freely went the extra mile for me in the pursuit of elusive illustrations, tracking down images from his own collection, as well as other sources. These have vastly improved the final work.

Richard S. Joslin is the great-grandson of Sylvester Marsh, who developed the concept of a cog railway and established its earliest practical use—at Mount Washington. Dick supplied the wonderful Marsh photograph and offered additional helpful encouragement and valuable food for thought. Of his own initiative, he patiently searched various Boston newspapers and surprised me with additional particulars he located.

Clergue T. Jones is the great-nephew of Francis H. Clergue, the central figure in the Green Mountain Railway story. He talked freely and at length about his unique, first-hand knowledge of the Clergue family, gladly relating and sharing the relevant portions he has painstakingly compiled and organized over the years.

Earle G. Shettleworth, Jr., Maine's renowned State Historian and longtime Director of the Maine Historic Preservation Commission, generously made available an invaluable selection of early photographs that have significantly complemented and enhanced the text. In addition, I owe him a deep debt of gratitude for reading and reviewing the manuscript.

Earl Brechlin is editor of the *Mount Desert Islander,* an important Bar Harbor newspaper. Also a registered Maine guide, he is an acknowledged authority on "MDI outdoors" and has written extensively on how to best experience the island, afoot and afloat. Earl gladly reviewed the manuscript, for which I am most thankful.

Ronald H. Epp, Ph.D., Director of the Shapiro Library at the Southern New Hampshire University, Manchester, N.H., is currently researching a scholarly biography of George B. Dorr, the extraordinary individual responsible for the creation and early success of Acadia National Park. Not surprisingly, our paths have crossed on several occasions. Ron unselfishly opened his voluminous files, which yielded countless nuggets of useful information. During several extended conversations, he repeatedly steered me toward additional resources that have likewise greatly benefited the final work.

Susan Smith, at the Bangor Public Library, did a masterful job of sleuthing, to unearth a variety of obscure images and information that otherwise would have eluded me.

Elaine Smith, in the Fogler Library's Special Collections Department at the University of Maine at Orono, was always extra-efficient whenever I called on her to locate and copy countless pages of useful documents and related material.

Dorothy Erikson, granddaughter of Daniel Brewer, an important figure in the early history of Green Mountain, graciously helped with key facts concerning the Brewer family, while her husband Gordon eagerly applied his capable photographic skills to make me a superb copy of an early Brewer portrait.

Harold E. Nelson, a longtime employee at the Maine Department of Transportation in Augusta, was the perfect source for details concerning the U. S. Coast Survey's early work at Green Mountain.

The wizardry and patience of Ollie, Fred, and Pac at Ollie's Imaging Service in Casco resulted in the successful rejuvenation of a host of timeworn images that otherwise would have been little more than indiscernible, if not wholly unusable.

Janet L. Patterson of Rockland has been a true joy to work with, as she imaginatively manipulated a medley of text and images through the highly involved design, layout, and production stages.

I also wish to profoundly thank the many other individuals who assisted me in an endless number of meaningful and beneficial ways. They include: Rebecca Cole-Will, Curator, and Julia Clark, Collections Manager, Abbe Museum, Bar Harbor; Brooke Childrey, Curator, and Tim Karle, Museum Technician, William Otis Sawtelle Collections & Research Center, Acadia National Park, Bar Harbor; Scott Proctor, Christine Riggle, and Tim Mahoney, Reference Staff, Baker Library, Harvard Business School, Cambridge, Massachusetts; Dana Lippitt, Curator,

Bangor Museum & Center for History, Bangor; David Rand, Chief, Bar Harbor Fire Department, Bar Harbor; Deborah M. Dyer, Curator, Bar Harbor Historical Society Museum, Bar Harbor; Dale R. Beeks, Mt. Vernon, Iowa; John Carleton Chapman, Westmont, Illinois; Chris C. Church, Portland; Eric Perkins, Ellsworth Photo Service, Ellsworth; Ellsworth Public Library, Ellsworth; Hale & Hamlin, Attorneys at Law, Ellsworth; Allan Ott, Hancock County Registry of Deeds, Ellsworth; Jesup Library, Bar Harbor; Rodney Laughton, Scarborough; William David Barry, Stephanie Philbrick, and Christine Albert, Maine Historical Society, Portland; Anthony Douin, Reference Services, Maine State Archives, Augusta; Susan McCarthy, Reference Librarian, Maine State Library, Augusta; Jane B. and Eugene D. Morin, Portland; Charlotte Singleton, Executive Director, and Rosamond S. Rea, Curator of Collections, Mount Desert Island Historical Society, Mount Desert; Patti Leland-Hanson, Editor, 2003 *Mount Desert Island History Journal*; Douglas H. Waites, Mount Washington Railway Company, Mt. Washington, New Hampshire; Marjorie Ciarlante, Civilian Records, National Archives and Records Administration, College Park, Maryland; Robert Pyle, Director, and Tina Hawes, Northeast Harbor Public Library, Mount Desert; Penobscot County Registry of Deeds, Bangor; Joe McCary, Photo Response Service, Gaithersburg, Maryland; Thomas Gaffney, Portland Public Library, Portland; Jaylene Roths; Heather Petingola, Sault Ste. Marie Chamber of Commerce, Sault Ste. Marie, Ontario; Kathryn Fisher, Director/Curator, Sault Ste. Marie Museum, Sault Ste. Marie, Ontario; Linda Burtch, Archivist, Sault Ste. Marie Public Library, Sault Ste. Marie, Ontario; Ben Proud, Special Collections Librarian, Fogler Library, University of Maine, Orono; Meredith Hutchins, Curator, Historic Photograph Collection, Southwest Harbor Public Library, Southwest Harbor; Mark Knierim, Reference Desk, State of Maine Law and Legislative Reference Library, Augusta;

Robert Shindle, Project Archivist, Steamship Historical Society of America, Baltimore, Maryland; Roger Woodfill, LS, Administrator, Surveyors Historical Society, Lawrenceburg, Indiana; Dodi Austin, Customer Service Representative, Union Trust Company, Ellsworth; Roger L. Payne, Executive Secretary, U. S. Board on Geographic Names, U. S. Geological Survey, Reston, Virginia; U. S. Patent and Trademark Office, Washington, D.C.; the U. S. Postal Service staff, Ellsworth; Roy C. Wells III, Wells Photographic, Randolph; and Joshua Torrance, Executive Director, Woodlawn Museum, Ellsworth. One especially helpful person has asked to remain anonymous, but cannot escape my particular thanks for repeated gracious service.

To all others who in any manner lent their time, knowledge, efforts, or support, yet I failed to mention them here, please forgive me. In short, I sincerely appreciate everyone's contributions, however great or small. I will not forget you, nor them.

Peter Dow Bachelder
Ellsworth, Maine
December 15, 2004

INTRODUCTION

Geology

Travel writers struggle to find words that adequately describe the primitive beauty preserved within Acadia National Park, a much-beloved jewel on Maine's island-strewn downeast coast. A sightseer's paradise and a naturalist's sanctuary, much of Acadia's twenty-two square miles sprawl across Mount Desert Island, which separates Blue Hill Bay to the southwest from Frenchman Bay to the northeast.

The area gained its present appearance during the last ice age. A developing glacier pressing southward out of eastern Canada gradually blanketed the region beneath thousands of feet of unyielding ice. Moving with imperceptible speed, the massive sheet methodically cut across a vast, hitherto-uninterrupted ridge—geologists call it a *peneplain*—known as the Mount Desert Range. In its wake the receding ice revealed an epic panorama of scarred granite mountains, interspersed with north-to-south U-shaped valleys. Across the rugged landscape occasional sparkling lakes and ponds attest to the glacier's scouring power and provide an added dimension to Acadia's widely esteemed loveliness.

Evidence of the glacier's overwhelming action is frequently visible as grooves and striations in the often-exposed ledges across the island. It also shows up in the form of large boulders (*erratics*), which the glacier plucked from the underlying bedrock. These were later haphazardly deposited, often miles away (including on sloping hillsides and mountaintops), when the ice blanket halted its further movement and melted. Less noticeable, but unmistakable, are the pockets of

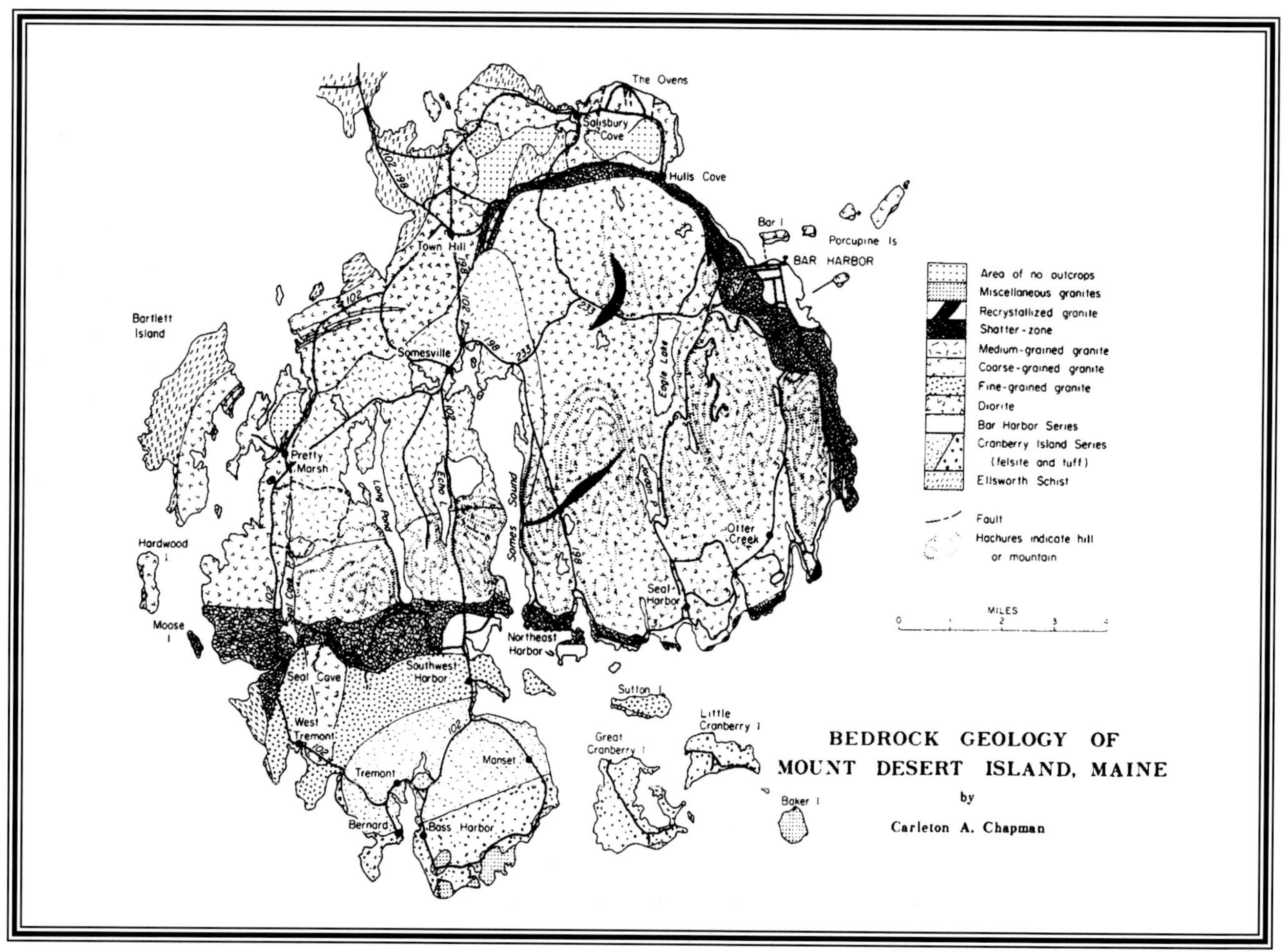

The Ovens
Salisbury Cove
Hulls Cove
Bar I
Porcupine Is
BAR HARBOR
Town Hill
Bartlett Island
Somesville
Eagle Lake
Pretty Marsh
Long Pond
Echo L.
Somes Sound
Otter Creek
Hardwood I
Seal Harbor
Moose I
Northeast Harbor
Seal Cove
Southwest Harbor
Sutton I
West Tremont
Little Cranberry I
Great Cranberry I
Manset
Tremont
Bernard
Bass Harbor
Baker I

Area of no outcrops
Miscellaneous granites
Recrystallized granite
Shatter-zone
Medium-grained granite
Coarse-grained granite
Fine-grained granite
Diorite
Bar Harbor Series
Cranberry Island Series
(felsite and tuff)
Ellsworth Schist

Fault
Hachures indicate hill
or mountain

MILES
0   1   2   3   4

BEDROCK GEOLOGY OF
MOUNT DESERT ISLAND, MAINE
by
Carleton A. Chapman

glacial debris—random mixtures of silt, sand, and pebbles known as *till*. Some have since been uncovered and utilized as gravel pits. Others remain where the material dropped, effectively preventing drainage from troughs to raise water levels or create areas of marsh and swamp.[1]

Today's landscape remains subjected to the constant forces of erosion and weathering, which continue the reshaping process. The seasonal freezing and melting of water in the cracks and crevices of coarse-grained granite outcrops cause slabs of rock to fracture into progressively smaller fragments. Similarly, at the meeting point of land and sea, the ocean's ever-restless movement constantly wears away projecting cliffs and headlands. Caught in the wash, the splintered rubble is dashed upon itself until it rounds into boulders or pebbles and eventually becomes sand.

Early MDI Inhabitants and Landowners

Archaeological evidence suggests that Native Americans lived on Mount Desert Island (MDI) as many as 6,000 years ago. During the last millennium ancestors of the modern Penobscot Nation dwelt here—fishing, hunting, harvesting shellfish, and gathering birch bark, berries, and sweet grass. Calling the place *Pemetic*, or "sloping land," they set up tight-knit villages along the sheltered shores and developed a self-sufficient, independent lifestyle that more than amply suited their fundamental needs.[2]

After centuries of maintaining a practical, peaceful culture, these indigenous coastal inhabitants one day found their long-established way of life permanently interrupted and ultimately ended by bold newcomers from western Europe—initially by daring explorers; later, would-be settlers.

Facing page:
The granite-ribbed mountains, majestic cliffs, and rugged shores that symbolize Mount Desert Island result from a timeless sequence of geologic upheavals, volcanic eruptions, and glacial erosion that have combined to create some of the most awe-inspiring scenery imaginable.

Courtesy of John Carleton Chapman, Westmont, Illinois

Facing page:

For thousands of years Native Americans inhabited compact shoreline communities on Mount Desert Island. This depiction of a summer encampment at Otter Creek is part of a more comprehensive diorama exhibited at the Abbe Museum, Sieur de Monts Springs, Acadia National Park.

Abbe Museum, Bar Harbor

History does not identify the first European to see or visit MDI. Although others before him may have at least glimpsed its distinctive contour, geographer/mapmaker Samuel de Champlain definitely set foot here in the late summer of 1604. Sailing a tiny, square-rigged ketch from the lower St. Croix River, a broad estuary that separates extreme eastern Maine from southwestern New Brunswick, Champlain had orders to explore and map the Maine coast on behalf of French royalist Pierre du Gua, Sieur de Monts.[3]

A favored officer in the royal household of Henry IV (king of France), de Monts had earlier visited French colonies bordering the St. Lawrence River in Canada. In late 1603 he received (from Henry) a charter for the entire North American territory between the fortieth and forty-sixth parallels. The following April, de Monts led an expedition to occupy the newly acquired realm. In late June he chose St. Croix Island as the site for the first French settlement on the Atlantic coast south of Cape Breton, in eastern Nova Scotia. While the work of establishing the de Monts colony moved forward, Champlain embarked on his coast-charting venture. On September 5, 1604, he and his party sailed into Frenchman Bay. Champlain's journal, translated from French, describes his initial impressions of today's Mount Desert Island:

> From this island to the mainland on the north, the distance is less than a hundred paces. It is very high, and notched in places, so that there is an appearance to one at sea, as of seven or eight mountains extending along near each other. The summits of the most of them are destitute of trees, as there are only rocks on them. The woods consist of pines, fir, and birches only.

French geographer Samuel de Champlain visited North America a dozen times during the first third of the seventeenth century. Between 1604 and 1607 he painstakingly explored and mapped the North Atlantic coast from the Bay of Fundy to Cape Cod.

Jesup Library, Bar Harbor

Champlain continued on, surveying as far south as the Kennebec River before returning to St. Croix Island, where he rejoined de Monts September 23. The attempted French colonization failed, due to harsh weather and a rampant outbreak of scurvy that claimed the lives of 35 of the 79 members in the company.[4]

After more than two years of futile searching for an alternate site for a permanent settlement, de Monts returned to France, where he later began conveying portions of the royal grant to interested parties. In 1613 Antoinette de Pons (Marquise de Guercheville) acquired the parcel that included MDI. Soon after, she dispatched a short-lived Jesuit mission at Fernald Point, on the south side of the island. It was aborted when Englishman Samuel Argall, who had been directed to remove any French settlements on the northeast coasts, surprised the French and scattered the colonists.

Over the next 150 years the English and French skirmished for possession of the region. In 1688 Antoine Laumet, the son of a French lawyer and an enterprising upstart seeking fame and fortune in North America, changed his name to "La Mothe" and began calling himself "Sieur de Cadillac," after a town near his birthplace. In 1687 Cadillac and his new wife sailed from France and arrived at MDI, where they stayed several months before moving to Montreal. Once across the border Cadillac obtained a grant from the governor of Canada for land fronting Frenchman Bay, including "the island of Mount Desert, and the other islands that are in the foreground . . . two leagues [the Cranberry Isles]." Cadillac apparently never returned to Maine, instead going on to found Detroit and become governor of French Louisiana. His departure essentially ended the reality of a permanent French settlement at MDI.[5]

By 1760 the convincing arguments of Francis Bernard, Royal Governor of the Province of Massachusetts Bay, helped settle the conflicting claims to the territory east of the Penobscot River in favor of the English. As a result Massachusetts, rather than Nova Scotia, gained full possession of MDI, and in 1764 Governor Bernard became the sole proprietor. Bernard was unable to satisfactorily manage the new holdings, and the English government ultimately replaced him as governor.

Following the American Revolution two claimants for Mount Desert Island came forward: Sir John Bernard, son of Francis; and Madame Marie Therese de Gregoire, granddaughter of Antoine Laumet, the self-proclaimed Sieur de Cadillac. Bernard petitioned the Massachusetts General Court to have the entire island restored to him, since it earlier had been his father's. Madame de Gregoire made a similar demand, citing her heritage. The Court ultimately accepted both claims, and de Gregoire took possession of the eastern half of the island (plus a tract of adjoining mainland), while the western portion went to Bernard.[6]

Madame de Gregoire subsequently went into debt, and on June 1, 1791, many of her holdings were conveyed to Henry Jackson of Boston. Jackson, in turn, sold out in July 1796 to Senator William Bingham, an immensely wealthy, influential Philadelphia banker.[7] Bingham already owned huge tracts of land in eastern Maine—ones he had either gained in a 1786 lottery conducted by the Commonwealth of Massachusetts, or obtained afterward from others who had participated in the drawing. Following Bingham's death in 1803 his assets were transferred to the Bingham Trust.[8]

The Summer People: Rusticators and the Elite

The first Caucasian settlers to Mount Desert Island began arriving in the early 1760s. Most ventured north from Cape Ann and Cape Cod, in Massachusetts,

On his arrival at Mount Desert Island in 1844, landscape painter Thomas Cole (left) was immediately captivated by the rugged beauty he encountered. The following summer he returned with an understudy, Frederic Church (right). The pair, with a growing stream of other enthusiastic artists, captured their impressions of the place in a series of highly acclaimed paintings that revealed its magnificence to a broad range of art lovers.

Library of Congress (left)
National Portrait Gallery, Smithsonian Institution (right)

and from various southwestern Maine communities—notably Arundel and Harpswell. Others migrated west from Nova Scotia. Before the end of the century they developed a working economy based on available natural resources—forest products (timber for lumber, shipbuilding, and cordwood) and marine harvests (fish and lobster). They built and sailed their own ships, grew their own crops, and manufactured their own staples. By 1850 they had utilized almost all the land that could be improved for growing crops or hay, or groomed as pasture, as well as every suitable site for a saw or grist mill.[9]

Prior to the 1840s, MDI inhabitants presumably took little, if any time to appreciate the attractiveness of their surroundings. The need for basic subsistence typically filled their every waking moment. As a result the beauties of the area went largely unnoticed for several decades. This changed dramatically after New Yorker Thomas Cole visited the island in 1844. Cole was the patriarch of the Hudson River School, a loose-knit group of landscape painters who found the American wilderness an appealing and compelling subject for their work. Cole came to MDI in September 1844, boarding at the Lynam farm at Schooner Head, south of Bar Harbor. Captivated by what he saw at every turn he returned the following summer for further exploration and work, bringing with him Frederic Edwin Church, one of his pupils.

Cole's contagious exuberance for the area prompted other fellow artists to visit. They fanned out across the island, painting and sketching a noteworthy collection of eye-catching Mount Desert scenery, done in a Romantic style of realism often enhanced with glowing sunlight, giving the works an almost ethereal luminescence. Exhibited at big city galleries throughout the northeast, the innovative, captivating canvases appealed to numerous affluent buyers who had the means to go and see the spectacular subjects for themselves—and soon did.

During their MDI visits the Hudson River artists stayed at local farmhouses, since there were no commercial lodgings on the eastern side of the island. In 1852 Albert Higgins of Bar Harbor formally opened his house for long-term visitors, earning the distinction of being the region's first hotelier. Higgins' early success encouraged some of his neighbors to likewise cater to the "summer colony." In 1855 Tobias Roberts established the Agamont House, overlooking the town pier. Three years later Captain Charles Deering erected the Deering House, a block up the street. The previous year Capt. Deering had begun offering regular, waterborne passenger service to Bar Harbor via the steamer *Rockland*, providing easier-than-ever access to an area even then experiencing the growing pains of a highly favored resort community.[10]

The Civil War (1861–1865) temporarily slowed the influx of Bar Harbor's summer guests, although it quickly accelerated afterward. The steady growth prompted a dramatic increase in the number of area lodgings. By 1872 no fewer than 15 hotels had sprung up in Bar Harbor and as many more in surrounding communities. A few evolved from early boarding houses; the rest were creations of enterprising locals quick to exploit the rapidly developing transient traveler market.

By the 1880s Bar Harbor had truly been "discovered" as a place of outstanding beauty and a preferred destination for a wide variety of outdoors enthusiasts. Visitors now included not only the pioneering artists and their immediate successors (educators, students, members of the clergy—i.e., those with ample free time), but increasing numbers of the elite. The earlier types, dubbed "rusticators," were typically younger and more active, the sort who desired little more than to experience first-hand the beauties and recreational opportunities the island afforded: hiking, fishing, boating, etc. For them, quality accommodations were unnecessary—and unwanted. The more recent arrivals were not so adventuresome, content to spend their days in less rigorous pursuits, including: reading, walking, going for meandering buckboard rides, and picnicking.

The hotel scene blossomed. Many of the earlier, unpretentious properties were significantly enlarged and adorned, the owners willingly adding rooms and amenities to suit guests' every whim. The Rodick House, constructed in 1866, underwent expansion on three separate occasions until, in 1882, it boasted six

By the 1880s Bar Harbor's tourist business was booming, and hotel operators were scrambling to provide for the arriving travelers' every need. The Rodick House began as an unassuming lodging in 1866 and quickly prospered to the extent that, in 1875, proprietor David Rodick enlarged it to accommodate 300 guests. Seven years later, further expansion resulted in a splendid, six-story edifice boasting more than 400 sleeping rooms.

Courtesy of Maine Historic Preservation Commission, Augusta

stories, 400 rooms, spacious music and dance halls and was touted the largest hotel in Maine.[11]

But not all the more affluent who came to Bar Harbor stayed in commercial lodgings. In 1868 Alpheus Hardy of Boston built his own summer place, where he could spend time in relative privacy. Hardy's "cottage" stood on Birch Point, near the site of today's Bar Harbor Motor Inn. Over the ensuing two decades a flourishing colony of summer visitors, some former boarders, purchased select, typically waterfront sites, where they erected quiet retreats quite apart from the relative hustle and bustle of the hotels. By 1890 this enclave included a broad mix of America's rich and famous, who vied with one another to put up the most luxurious estates imaginable. The aristocrats developed their own whirlwind social scene, opening their mansions to entertain one another (and countless invited guests) via sumptuous banquets, lavish dances and cotillions, and quality musical entertainment. They also established exclusive associations, including the Oasis Club, the Canoe Club, and the Kebo Valley Club, among others, where the various fashionable activities of the day—canoeing, tennis, lawn croquet, and golf—flourished.

The 1880s brought rapid advancement to Bar Harbor's once-simplistic infrastructure: electricity, telephones, a fire department, and a public water/sewer system. Opportunities for further sorts of leisure activity appeared, as well: a theater, museum, race track, roller-skating rink, bowling alley, baseball field, and tennis courts. Bar Harbor had come of age.

Such rapid-fire changes typically produce unanticipated controversy within an otherwise harmonious community, and Bar Harbor's explosive, socioeconomic transition yielded its own disruptive moment. The surprising catalyst was a young Bangor chap whose progressive ideas and mostly unwelcome plans created an immediate stir among residents and cottagers alike, prompting them to forge a sizable constituency that would ultimately set the tone for shaping the future long-term growth and development of the island.[12]

 CHAPTER ONE

Green Mountain

A Coastal Landmark

At 1,532 feet above sea level the summit of Cadillac Mountain is the loftiest spot on Mount Desert Island. Moreover, it holds the distinction of being the second highest point on the immediate western shores of the Atlantic Ocean. Only 2,310-foot Mount Corcovado, at Rio de Janeiro, Brazil, is taller.[1]

For as long as mariners have sailed the Maine coast, Cadillac's broad profile has been a welcome landmark. Long before the first lighted aids to navigation, ships along the transatlantic route crossing the Gulf of Maine guided on its prominent peak, which in clear weather is visible 35 to 45 miles offshore.[2] For centuries, countless coasting vessels have found its presence helpful, if not downright indispensable.

Mention of MDI occurs early in recorded history. Samuel de Champlain's 1607 map denotes it as "I. des Monts deserts" (Island of the barren mountains).[3] In Governor John Winthrop's *Journal* of 1630 are the first known sketches of the island, made June 8 when he sighted the highest peaks well to the northwest, while sailing between Nova Scotia and Massachusetts.[4] During the mid-eighteenth

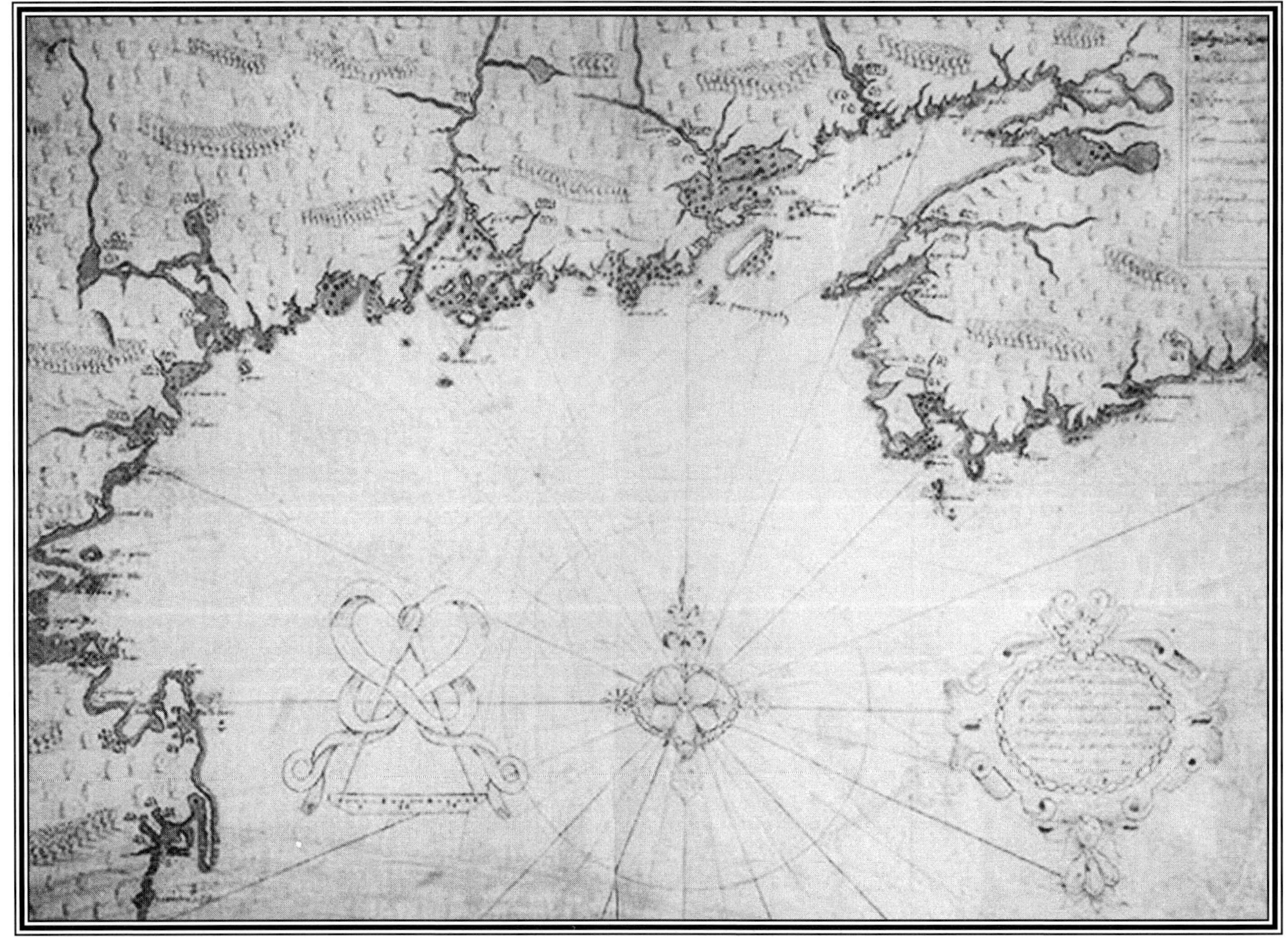

century, references to MDI began to appear in atlases and sailing directions and on marine charts. The 1706 Mount edition of *The English Pilot, The Fourth Edition,* a much-used British sea-atlas published from 1671 to 1803, includes it, as do all succeeding versions.[5] In 1765 the Massachusetts General Court had the entire Maine coast surveyed and afterward brought out a map depicting an accurate outline of MDI and the neighboring islands.[6] In 1772 engineer and hydrographer Samuel Holland, official British surveyor of the U.S. coast north of the Potomac River, made a series of charts of the Maine and New England coasts, including ones showing MDI.[7] They subsequently appeared in British Army engineer Joseph F. W. Des Barres' monumental *Atlantic Neptune,* an immense collection of painstakingly detailed navigational charts embodying much of the east coast of North America.[8]

Although the name "Mount Desert Island" has deep roots, the earliest records identifying today's Cadillac Mountain occur much later. In John & James Peters' *Survey of the De Gregoire half of the Island, 1807,* it appears as "Bauld."[9] New York lawyer Charles Tracy, in the diary of his family's 1855 visit to MDI, called it "Newport" (also a former name for nearby Champlain Mountain).[10] By the 1860s "Green" had become widely accepted, showing up on H. F. Walling's 1860 *Topographic Map of Hancock Co.,*[11] as well as in two early, popular guidebooks: Clara Barnes Martin's *Mount Desert on the Coast of Maine,* originally written in late 1866,[12] and Benjamin F. DeCosta's 1871 *Rambles In Mount Desert.*[13] During the creation of Lafayette (later Acadia) National Park, federal officials in 1918 agreed that "Cadillac" was a more appropriate designation and so renamed it. Area residents strongly opposed the change. Noted maritime historian and longtime MDI summer resident Samuel Eliot Morison, in his 1930 essay "The Course of the *Arabella* from Cape Sable to Salem," steadfastly referred to it as "Green,"

Facing page:

Champlain's 1607 map, including the Maine coast, was the first to identify Mount Desert Island, labeling it "I. des Mont Deserts" (Island of the barren mountains).

Library of Congress

pausing after the first mention to parenthetically insert "absurdly renamed Cadillac." Morison was not alone in his sentiment. An early 1931 readers' poll in the weekly *Bar Harbor Times* determined that 98 percent of the more than 200 respondents preferred "Green."[14]

Apparently the renaming controversy remained a thorn in Morison's side. On May 27, 1931, he wrote a somewhat pointed letter to Secretary of the Interior Harold L. Ickes, requesting the name "Green" and those of several other redesignated Acadia peaks be restored. Morison began by brashly stating that "many names of the mountains, which are a conspicuous feature of this island, were changed, because a small group of busybodies thought that the old ones were too homely, and got the ear of the then Secretary of the Interior." Perhaps with knowledge of the recent *Times'* survey in mind, he further declared, "those who love the island deeply resent the change" and went on to say, "residents are pretty tired of tourist wits asking, 'Where are Chevrolet, Ford, and Packard Mountains?'" Morison's plea was politely considered, but denied.[15]

Earliest Visitors to the Summit

Native Americans were arguably the first people to reach the top of Cadillac Mountain. The early natives typically scaled the summit via the more-gently-sloping north and south ridges, rather than the steeper east and west faces. They were not interested in a challenging climb, desiring only to arrive at their destination without damaging the landscape, which they revered. They likewise preferred to avoid obstacles, rather than harm them, and would go out of their way to do so.[16]

In 1866 Daniel Brewer had a rough carriage road constructed up the north ridge of Green Mountain, enabling horse-drawn buggies and buckboards to reach the broad, open summit.

Bar Harbor Historical Society

The course of the ancient, aboriginal trail along Cadillac's north ridge was essentially the same one a crude, mid-nineteenth century buckboard road followed. The latter commenced at the Eagle Lake Road, then passed just west of the top of Great Pond Hill and slightly east of The Whitecap, the two most prominent eminences along the mountain's sprawling flank. Over the final mile the early thoroughfare straddled the granite-capped ridgeline, as it angles upward roughly 500 feet to the summit.[17]

The name of the first western European to scale Cadillac (hereafter referred to as "Green") is unknown, as is the date of the effort. The daring adventurer likely followed much the same route as the Natives who had made the trek for countless centuries.

Green Mountain Ownership

In 1847 John D. Gilmore, of Ellsworth, and Edward Brewer, an enterprising shipbuilder and aspiring lumber baron at Hull's Cove, purchased several parcels of island real estate, including the summit of Green Mountain, from the Bingham estate, with an eye toward harvesting the rich stands of timber they contained. A year later Gilmore sold his portion to Brewer. In 1857 Edward Brewer's sons, Daniel, Perry and Porter, acquired the parcel containing Green Mountain's summit.[18]

George Bucknam Dorr was the driving force behind the creation of Acadia National Park. In 1908 he learned that the Brewers had been approached by local interests wanting to acquire the rights to the timber that grew on their lands—specifically, in the higher elevations of MDI's eastern peaks. Dorr hastily arranged to acquire the property in question, to prevent it from being clear-cut. Eight years later he was instrumental in having it, together with several thousand acres of related holdings, transferred to the ownership of the federal government, which presently administers the entire parcel as Acadia National Park.[19]

The U.S. Coast Survey

In 1807 President Thomas Jefferson created the Survey of the Coast, a federal agency mandated to—among other scientific responsibilities—chart and map

A great-grandson of Benjamin Franklin, Philadelphia-born Alexander Dallas Bache *(left)* (1806–1867) became one of the most respected American scientists of the mid-nineteenth century. In 1843 he accepted the position of Superintendent of the U. S. Coast Survey, a post he held until his death. Under his leadership, survey teams mapped and charted most U. S. coastal waters, including those in Maine.

In August 1853, U. S. Coast Survey assistant Charles O. Boutelle *(right)* supervised the establishment of a signal station atop Green Mountain. For the next several years the site played a vital role in the task of gathering data associated with creating accurate hydrographic charts of the Maine coast.

Library of Congress (left)
National Archives (right)

America's coastline. Renamed the U. S. Coast Survey in 1836, the organization achieved its most notable accomplishments under the leadership of its second superintendent, Alexander Dallas Bache, who assumed control in 1843. Under Bache's direction the necessary fieldwork took place that paved the way for mapping the coast of Maine.[20]

One of the preliminary steps in the Coast Survey's charting process involved selecting sites for primary triangulation stations, where accurate measurements of distance and direction could be determined. One of the requisites for each location was that it have a direct line-of-sight to surrounding stations. Much of the primary triangulation in Maine was carried out at the summits of mountains, which were ideally suited for the work and allowed observations across greater distances than were possible elsewhere along the east coast.[21] Green Mountain was among more than a half-dozen spots similarly selected.

During the summer of 1853 Coast Survey specialist Thomas McDonnell led a crew that carved out a primitive road to the summit of Green Mountain, up which a team of horses could haul equipment and materials. Richard Hamor of Bar Harbor was hired to build "in a sheltered place near the top . . . (a) house 10 x 12 square, & 9 feet high of boards battened with 3 x 1 inch battens on the roof and sides, floored with table & 2 bunks inside, to have one window with 8 lights and a sliding shutter or deadlight outside to secure it." Hamor was paid $50 for the effort.[22] The rude hut served to shelter a Coast Survey triangulation crew and provided a place for their gear and provisions.

On August 6, 1853, Charles O. Boutelle, one of Alexander Bache's assistants, established a working signal for "station Mount Desert" (as contemporary Coast Survey documents referred to it), mounted on a tall, skeletal wooden tripod. From the crotch of the structure's spruce framework rose a 17.5-foot pole, reinforced by 27- and 30-foot braces. The slender column was painted black with a four-foot, white band slightly more than halfway up. At the top a rotating apparatus known as a "heliotrope" utilized a tin mirror that reflected the sun's rays and directed them as a narrow cone of light toward a given, distant point. Remote observers, often 20 miles or more away, focused on the beams to determine precise angles needed in drafting dependable maps and charts.[23] The instrument's operator, called a "heliotroper," communicated with surrounding stations using "heliography," a primitive language consisting of reflected impulses produced by a second mirror.

A "heliotrope" is an instrument that reflects and directs the sun's rays to a distant observer. Nineteenth century engineers used them during triangulation surveys to reveal their locations to distant observers, so the latter could determine precise angles needed in mapping projects. This model is similar to the one survey crews used at the summit of Green Mountain during the 1850s.

Courtesy of NOAA Library

In 1855 a Coast Survey crew established a triangulation station atop 1,233-foot Mount Harris, in Dixmont, southwest of Bangor. Although the signal was placed on a masonry foundation 20 feet above the station mark, it still wasn't high enough to clear 1,062-foot Mount Waldo, in Frankfort, and link with the Green Mountain location. The following year Superintendent Bache supervised a team that erected a new scaffolding on Green Mountain, raising the Mount Desert signal to 56 feet above the foundation ledge and enabling the two stations to communicate.[24]

Coast Survey personnel utilized the Green Mountain location on a seasonal basis through 1860, when its established function was no longer necessary. The site continued to be used as late as 1865, principally for secondary triangulation purposes in connection with creating hydrographic charts of Frenchman Bay.[25]

The Mountain House

In 1866 prominent Hulls Cove landowner Daniel Webster Brewer built a small hotel atop Green Mountain.[26] Following a portion of the 1853 government trail he constructed a passable buckboard road to the summit, where he operated what Benjamin F. DeCosta's *Rambles in Mount Desert* guidebook describes as:

> . . . a rough-built structure, thrown together on the umbrella principle, with all the framework showing on the inside, being braced up without by light timbers of spruce planted in the rock to enable it to withstand the heavy gales. The little parlor in the center is flanked by the dining-room, and a couple of dormitories, while overhead, in the loft, a double tier of berths is arranged, steamboat fashion. . .[27]

Referred to in early deeds as the "Mountain House,"[28] the simple lodging was also variously called the "Green Mountain House,"[29] the "Summit House,"[30] and the "Tip Top House."[31] D. H. Swan managed the property during the early 1870s and reported that in 1874, some 3,000 people visited the mountaintop.[32] After Swan decided to run the Hamor House in Bar Harbor, the Mountain House continued to do business, although not always on a regular basis. In 1882 A. M. McQuinn kept the place, registering 1,900 visitors.[33]

As his father, Edward, before him, Hulls Cove native Daniel Brewer (1829–1895) was a prosperous shipbuilder/lumber baron and a prominent MDI landowner. His extensive holdings included the summit of Green Mountain, where in 1866 he built a primitive hotel called the Mountain House.

Courtesy of Dorothy and Gordon Erikson, Bar Harbor

Daniel Brewer's Mountain House operated through the early 1880s, offering simple, but hearty meals and modest overnight lodging. During the 1870s as many as 3,000 visitors patronized the place each summer.

Acadia National Park's William Otis Sawtelle Research and Collections Center, Bar Harbor

In 1882, the Mountain House's final year in business, A.M. McQuinn served as proprietor and hosted 1,900 guests.

Jesup Library, Bar Harbor

GREEN MOUNTAIN HOUSE,

Located on the summit of Green Mountain

BAR HARBOR, - MAINE.

A. M. McQUINN, PROPRIETOR.

Now open and ready to furnish Dinners and Luncheons.

The carriage road is in good condition for teams.

☞ The small fee collected at the summit is expended in keeping the carriage road in repair.

The Winds of Change

Over the years Daniel Brewer's buckboard road deteriorated to the extent that by the early 1880s some stretches had become almost impassable.[34] At the same time, summer visitors to MDI were swelling the local population many times over, and the lure of Green Mountain was annually drawing thousands—most of them climbers. During the summer of 1881 the *Mount Desert Herald*, Bar Harbor's pioneer newspaper, periodically mentioned Green Mountain's popularity. On August 4 one of the local interest items pointed out that on the previous day, more than 100 had enjoyed time at the summit.[35] Two weeks later a similar account indicated that 250 had done so on the 11th.[36] To those with an interest in the island's burgeoning recreation industry, it was becoming increasingly apparent that the mountain could be the island's premier tourist attraction, if only there were an easier way to reach the top. One of these was a far-sighted Bangor man, whose dreams included making MDI accessible to the world and Green Mountain a must-see spot once they arrived. An unknown to most island residents in 1882, within a year the name Francis H. Clergue would not only be familiar, but the most talked about—and controversial—in the community.

CHAPTER TWO

Francis H. Clergue and the Green Mountain Railway

Francis Clergue: The Formative Years

Francis Hector Clergue was born August 28, 1856, in Brewer, Maine. His father, Joseph Hector Clergue, had emigrated from Lorient, in the Bretagne region of France, in 1847 and eventually settled in the Bangor area, becoming a successful barber and wigmaker. His mother, Frances Clarissa Lombard, came from a family with deep Colonial roots; her father was David Sawyer Lombard, a renowned master shipbuilder.[1] Francis was the eldest of eight siblings—three boys and five girls—including a sister who died in infancy.[2]

After graduating from Bangor High School in 1875, Frank (as he was typically called during his adult years) enrolled at Maine State College (today's University of Maine) in Orono, but dropped out after a year and a half. In 1877 he wrote to Maine Senator Hannibal Hamlin, imploring the powerful politician to give him a position as private secretary in the latter's Washington office. The letter went unanswered. Undaunted, Clergue became a clerk for attorney Frederick M. Laughton in Bangor, where practical experience and self-education led to his becoming a partner in Laughton's firm. In 1884 he was named Bangor's City Solicitor.[3]

During the early 1880s Frank Clergue (as he was commonly called) abandoned a budding Bangor legal career to pursue a series of ambitious speculative ventures. One of the earliest was the construction of a cog railroad to the summit of Green Mountain, at Bar Harbor.

Courtesy of Bangor Public Library

Joseph H. Clergue arrived in Maine around 1850 and became a successful Bangor barber and wigmaker. He and his wife, the former Clarissa Lombard, raised seven children in a house on State Street. The eldest was a son, Francis Hector, who would make the Clergue name familiar in wide-ranging parts of the world. This ad appeared in the 1866 Bangor City Directory.

Courtesy of Bangor Public Library

Despite the early accomplishments Clergue soon became disenchanted with legal and administrative work, finding them interesting and challenging, but far too mundane. A resourceful person, Clergue was highly energetic; one family member described him as "a dynamo."[4] He was also a man of great insight and vision and would eventually champion a long string of speculative ventures that were his real consuming passion.

One of Frank Clergue's early fascinations was the generation and transmission of electric power, most notably with methods of harnessing it for industrial and commercial use. One application that particularly intrigued him was urban transportation—more specifically, an electric railroad. Clergue was apparently drawn

Incorporated in 1887, the Bangor Street Railway began service April 29, 1889, along a three-mile stretch between the East Hampden town line and the intersection of State and Pearl Streets, north of the city center. Frank Clergue, who stimulated early interest in the railroad project, served as the company's initial treasurer. Car No. 12, Maine's earliest electric trolley, was the first to operate on the line. Standing alongside the 16-foot box, built in Newburyport, Massachusetts, are motorman O'Brien and conductor Coombs.

Courtesy of Richard R. Shaw, Bangor

A prominent figure in late nineteenth century Bangor municipal circles, attorney Frederick M. Laughton was the city's mayor in 1875. Later he became the first president of the Bangor Electric Light & Power Company (today's Bangor Hydro-Electric Company), and was an influential member of the Green Mountain Railway's board of directors.

Courtesy of Local History/Special Collections, Bangor Public Library

to early experiments in the field by the prolific inventor Thomas A. Edison, best known for the development, in 1879, of the first commercially practical, incandescent lamp. While not the electric railroad's creator, Edison made several functional refinements to the basic concept between 1880 and 1882, before stopping further work for lack of financial support.[5] It would be Connecticut-born Frank J. Sprague who created the prototype that soon made the entire idea feasible. Sprague, a short-term Edison employee, ultimately developed a successful system of electric traction that led to the first citywide, electric street railway system in the United States—at Richmond, Virginia, in the spring of 1888.[6]

Although his role in the project has largely been overlooked, Frank Clergue was the first to advocate the idea of an electric street railway in Bangor, as well as the need for a hydroelectric plant to generate sufficient power for its widespread use. He was also instrumental in persuading law partner Frederick Laughton and a circle of Laughton's influential business associates to pursue the start-up, in 1885, of the Bangor Electric Power & Light Company and, five years later, the Veazie Hydro Station, on the Penobscot River, above Bangor.[7] Before the inception of either pioneering endeavor, however, Clergue had already conceived and laid the groundwork for an even more sensational undertaking—the creation of an electric railway on Mount Desert Island, spearheaded by the construction of a cog railroad up the rugged granite slopes of Green Mountain.

Clergue's Plan Unfolds

Customarily, entrepreneurs with bold new plans announce them with the greatest possible fanfare and gusto. The strategy is to draw all possible attention to the plan and gain the public's immediate, ongoing interest and approval. However, this was not the case with the beginnings of Frank Clergue's MDI railroad project, whose unveiling was at least a partial—and not an especially pleasant—surprise for most Bar Harbor-area residents. When word did come, the earliest particulars were scanty, and additional details appeared only sporadically, at least until proposals for actual work on the cog railroad appeared in the local newspaper.

The December 7, 1882, issue of the *Mount Desert Herald* carried the following tidbit in the "Local Interest Notes" column: "It is said that a party of capitalists have taken the preliminary steps for building a railroad from Bar Harbor to Green Mountain, and also contemplate the erection of a large hotel at the summit. Wonder who they are."

The suppositions were true, as more specific news a month later confirmed. In early January 1883 the *Herald* carried word that "two gentlemen from Bangor . . . are surveying Green Mountain for a projected railroad." The piece concluded with the editorial comment: ". . . we sincerely regret that our own people should let chances like these slip them and pass into the hands of outsiders."[8]

At this point the *Herald* had not yet fully grasped most islanders' (and nonresident property holders') real sentiments on the matter. The latters' chief concern was not that intruding "outsiders" would seize the opportunity to capitalize on such a brash undertaking; they were simply opposed to its very existence in the first place. And they would ultimately make these feelings altogether apparent.

Local reaction aside, as additional information emerged regarding Frank Clergue's railroad project, it soon became evident the plan was well conceived, had received strong financial backing, and was already well on the way to becoming a reality. In November 1882 Clergue formed the Green Mountain Railway Company and had it incorporated, with capital totaling $90,000. In addition to Clergue and Frederick Laughton, the project's major investors were mostly

The major investors in the Green Mountain Railway (GMR) were prominent Maine businesspeople. In addition to Frank Clergue and Frederick Laughton they included: (top row, left to right) Charles F. Bragg, senior partner, N. H. Bragg Co., Bangor *(Bangor Daily News)*; Sumner Laughton, Bangor physician/ophthalmic surgeon *(Local History/Special Collections, Bangor Public Library)*; Charles V. Lord, president, Veazie National Bank *(Local History/Special Collections, Bangor Public Library)*; William B. Hayford, president, Kenduskeag National Bank *(Bangor Daily News)*; (bottom row, left to right) Franklin W. Cram, superintendent, European & North American Railway *(Maine State Library, Augusta)*; Thomas N. Egery, co-owner, Hinckley & Egery Iron Company *(Local History/Special Collections, Bangor Public Library)*; Payson Tucker, president, Eastern and Maine Central Railroad *(Bangor Public Library)*

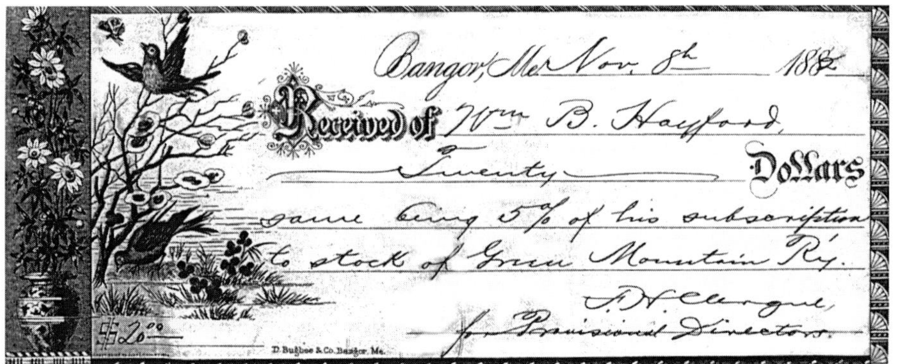

This receipt, dated November 8, 1882, was given to Bangor's William B. Hayford in exchange for a $20 payment toward the purchase of $400 in stock in the Green Mountain Railway. The voucher is signed "F. H. (Francis) Clergue."

Fogler Library Special Collections, University of Maine, Orono

Bangor businessmen and included: Charles F. Bragg, William B. Hayford, Sumner Laughton, Charles V. Lord, Thomas N. Egery, Franklin W. Cram, and Payson Tucker. Hayford was named company president, with Clergue appointed secretary, treasurer, and superintendent. The board of directors consisted of: Hayford, Lord, (Frederick) Laughton, Cram, Egery, and Clergue.[9]

A New Hampshire Inspiration

To some, the concept of a mountain-climbing locomotive might have seemed preposterous, except for the fact the mechanics of it were already a reality and being successfully employed in New Hampshire, thanks to Granite State native and entrepreneur Sylvester Marsh. One of eleven children growing up in Campton, in the central portion of the state, Marsh left home at the age of 19 and walked to Boston, where he worked at various jobs in the packaging trades.

Following a nearly disastrous hike up Mount Washington in August 1857, New Hampshire-born Sylvester Marsh (1803–1884) vowed to find an "easier and safer" way to reach the summit. His efforts resulted in the invention of the inclined railroad, which began operating commercially in 1869 as the Mount Washington Railway.

Courtesy of Richard S. Joslin, Cambridge, Massachusetts

Going on to Chicago in 1833, he amassed a fortune in the meat-packing business and gained further acclaim after discovering a way to keep grain—particularly corn—from spoiling while in long-term storage.[10]

Determined to slow the hectic pace of his busy life and enjoy more time with his wife and four children, Marsh retired to New England in 1855 and settled in Massachusetts. In August 1857 he spent time hiking with a friend in New Hampshire's White Mountains. On the upper slopes of Mount Washington the pair encountered a sudden, savage storm that almost cost them their lives. Freezing rain, hurricane-force winds, and early darkness nearly kept the two climbers from reaching the welcome shelter of the summit's 1853 Tip Top House. Badly shaken by the experience, Marsh resolved to find "some easier and safer method of ascension" to the pinnacle of New England's mightiest mountain. His solution would be revolutionary—a mountain-climbing locomotive![11]

Sylvester Marsh knew that smooth, round locomotive wheels could not grip conventional rails well enough to drive an engine up anything more than a slight grade. Adapting a concept originally developed in 1812 by Englishman John Blenkinsop, Marsh received, in 1861, a patent for a locomotive fitted with a cogwheel that turned in a toothed, central rail. A ratchet attached to the cog kept it from rotating backward during the locomotive's ascent, while a gripper beneath the central rail prevented the cog from disengaging. Three years later he obtained an additional patent for an air brake, necessary to slow the train during descent. Following further refinements to the cog rail and repeated tests with a working model, Marsh felt ready to put his remarkable invention to practical use.[12]

Beginning in April 1866 Sylvester Marsh supervised crews constructing a 2.8-mile rail line up Mount Washington's western slopes. Consisting of a wooden trestle supporting the central and outer rails, the railway averaged a 25 percent

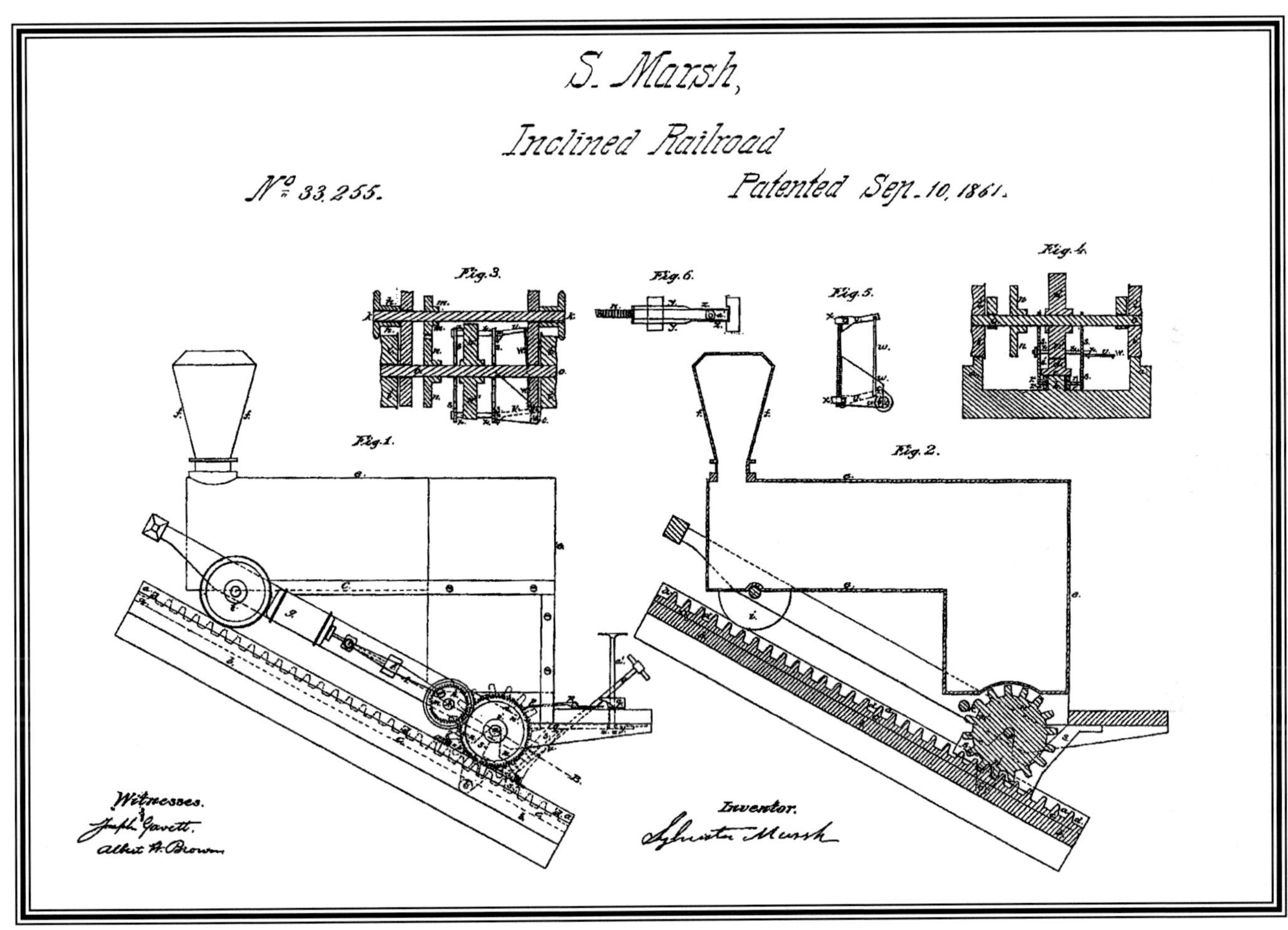

In 1858 Sylvester Marsh submitted plans for an inclined railroad to the U.S. Patent Office. Three years later the agency acknowledged the work as original and approved a copyright.

U.S. Patent Office

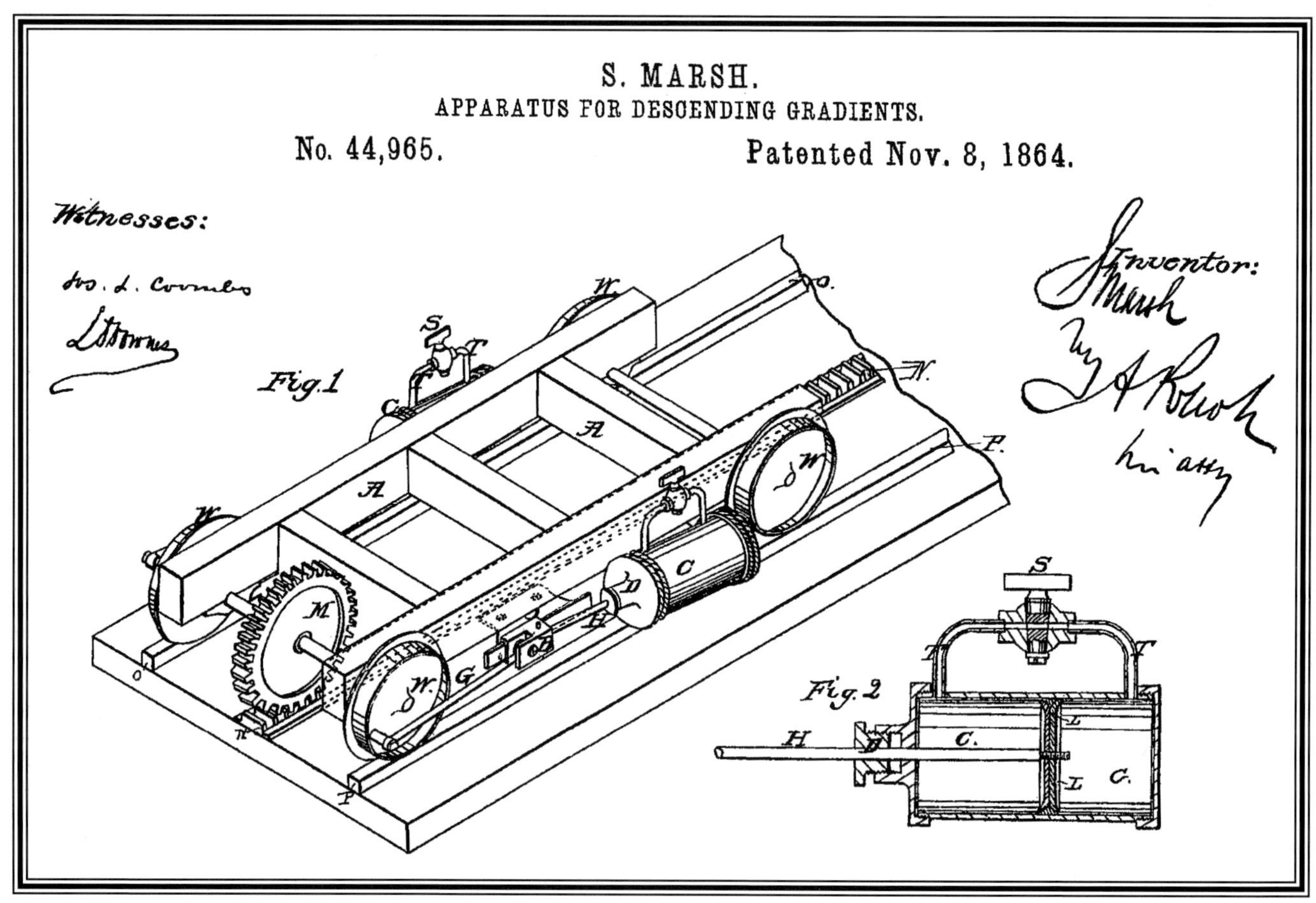

In 1864 Sylvester Marsh was granted a patent for an "Apparatus for Descending Gradients"—an adjustable, frictionless brake that utilized compressed air to slow a train's movement, while eliminating the wear and tear on a locomotive's (and/or carriage's) wheels.

U.S. Patent Office

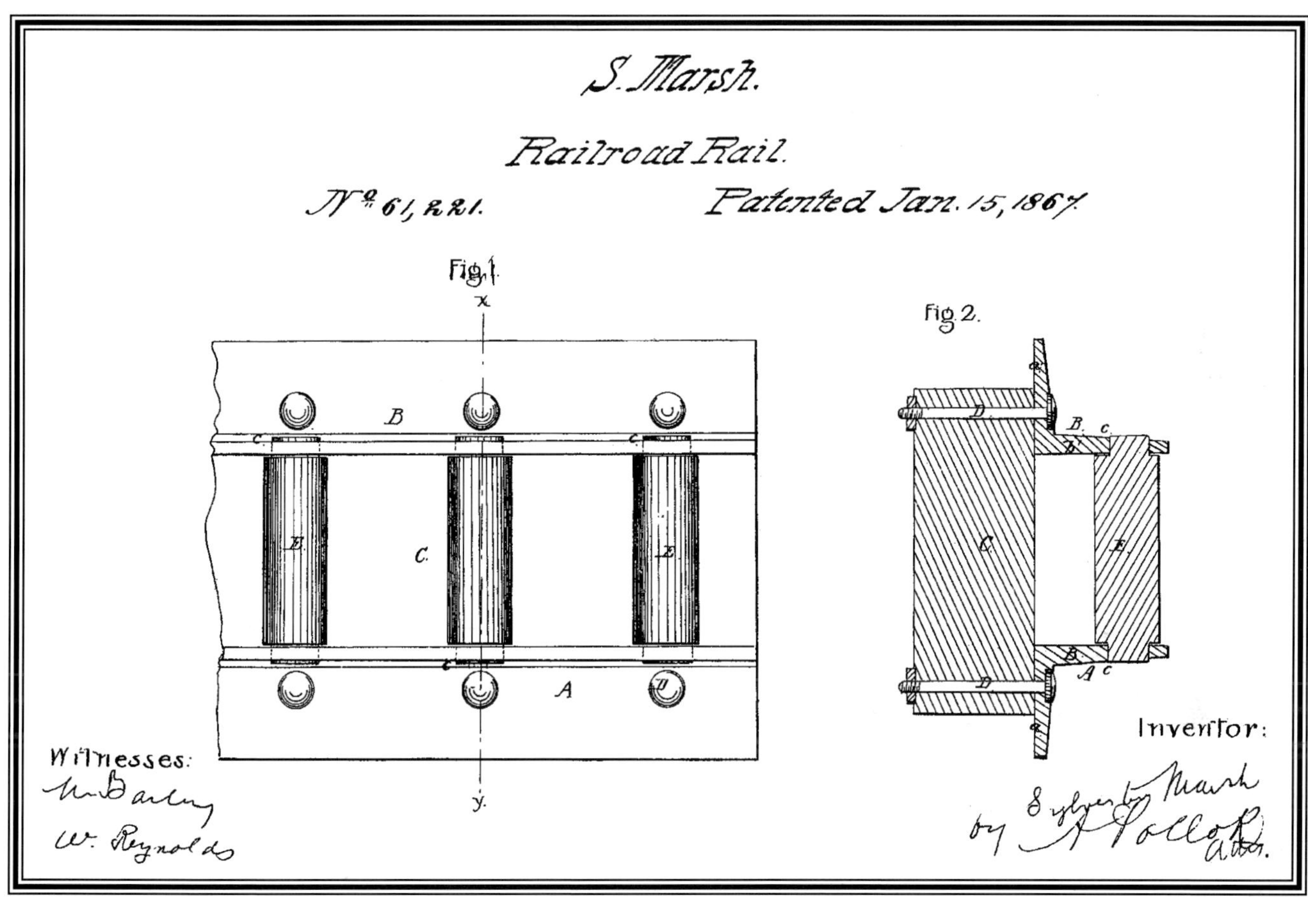

Sylvester Marsh also improved—and in January 1867 received a patent for—an enhanced design for the original cog rail. Marsh's device was "open" between the individual pins along the rack, and this allowed ice, snow, or dirt to fall through the spaces, rather than clog and potentially impede the works.

grade, while climbing the 3,625 vertical feet from the Marshfield base station to the 6,288-foot summit. The first train to reach the top arrived July 3, 1869, and the pioneering Mount Washington Railway (MWR) was born. More remarkably, it continues operating today. During the initial full season approximately 5,000 passengers rode the tiny train to the rooftop of New England. That number has grown to today's annual average of 70,000. In 1976 the railway was designated a National Historic Landmark.[13]

Determining the Railroad's Route

Aware of the Mount Washington Railway's immediate popular appeal, Frank Clergue was determined to establish a similar venture at Bar Harbor and make it—with Green Mountain as the showpiece—the area's foremost tourist attraction. He was fully aware of Bar Harbor's recent meteoric rise as a select travel destination, as well as the fact that during the previous five years several thousand people had annually trekked to Green Mountain's summit. He reasoned the numbers would increase dramatically once his railroad was in business.

On January 22, 1883, Clergue negotiated a 20-year lease with Daniel Brewer, Perry Brewer, and Orient W. Carpenter for 200 acres atop Green Mountain, plus a perpetual right-of-way for a 96-foot-wide strip from the base to the top, at a location of his choosing. In return Clergue agreed to pay the trio $100, one year from that date, then on every January 22 thereafter, five cents for each person visiting the summit during the previous twelve months. As part of the deal Clergue also acquired: (1) a 40-foot-wide right-of-way for horses, carriages, foot passengers, and railway along the east shore of Eagle Lake, between the Eagle Lake Road

On August 29, 1866, Sylvester Marsh conducted a successful demonstration at Mount Washington, proving to even the strongest detractors that his plan to build and operate a cog railroad to the summit of New England's highest mountain would work. The steam-driven locomotive *Hero* easily moved groups of railroad officials and other invited guests up and down a section of sloping track. After someone in the crowd commented how *Hero*'s upright boiler looked like a peppersauce bottle, the little locomotive quickly inherited the moniker *Peppersass.*

Courtesy of Randall H. Bennett

and the base of the railroad; (2) the unrestricted use (for a steamboat landing) of any wharves or piers built on the shores of Eagle Lake; and (3) the right to construct and use a wharf not over 50 feet wide on the shore side of the right-of-way. The full particulars are spelled out in a lease recorded June 6, 1883, at the Hancock County Registry of Deeds in Ellsworth.[14]

One of Clergue's first tasks was to determine the exact path the proposed railroad would follow. In December 1882 he hired two Bangor men, Alden F. Hilton and Captain Frank W. Goodwin, to explore Green Mountain's rocky slopes and select the most advantageous course for laying the track. In 1871 Hilton had engineered construction of the broad-gauge European & North American Railway, between Bangor and St. John, New Brunswick. Goodwin was one of GMR's stockholders.[15] Clergue also tapped Hilton to oversee the job of building the Green Mountain Railway, and Hilton did draw up a general plan. Before any meaningful work began, however, Hilton withdrew to manage a larger project—construction of the Megantic Railway connecting Montreal and Portland. Clergue then placed Franklin Cram in charge of the overall construction.[16] He also named Orrington's Warren Nickerson the chief engineer; George Jones, superintendent of laying the track; and Captain Goodwin, railroad superintendent.[17]

During December 1882 and early January 1883, Hilton and Goodwin explored the ice-and-snow-covered sides of Green Mountain, enduring several days of sub-zero conditions in the process. The pair ultimately chose a route beginning at the southeast shore of Eagle Lake and stretching 6,300 feet (1.2 miles) up the mountain's wooded west slope. The course was nearly straight, incorporating just two right-hand curves, each about 30 degrees.[18] Because the surface of Eagle Lake is 274 feet above sea level and Green Mountain's summit elevation is 1,532 feet, the total vertical ascent amounted to 1,258 feet. The average rise of the railbed would be one foot for every 4.5 feet traveled (roughly 22 degrees), while the steepest grade would gain nearly one foot in three (about 30 degrees).

Getting State Approval

Before Frank Clergue could formally establish the Green Mountain Railway, he needed official approval. In January 1883 he asked the Maine legislature for a charter "to build a railroad from the village of Bar Harbor to some point on Eagle Lake." Interestingly, no hard evidence exists that lawmakers in Augusta approved the request—i.e., Maine public laws do not include any such statute. Nonetheless, GMR did fully comply with the requirements set forth in the state's 1876 act authorizing the formation of railroad corporations: raising sufficient capital stock; naming appropriate company directors; creating valid, subscribed articles of association, etc.[19] The notarized document detailing the articles of association was signed by GMR officials on November 9, 1882, approved six days later by the Maine Board of Railroad Commissioners, and recorded in the Secretary of State's office November 23.[20]

Clergue also sought and received legislative approval to change the railroad's gauge (the distance between the two rails), so it would match the slightly narrower tracks used by the Mount Washington Railway. MWR's gauge measured four feet, seven and one-half inches, one inch less than the standard mandated by Congress in 1873. On February 3, 1883, Maine lawmakers passed a public and special law authorizing the Green Mountain Railway to adopt any gauge "not less than two feet nor more than six feet."[21] The ruling would allow Clergue to

George N. Colby's 1887 *Atlas of the State of Maine* includes a map of Bar Harbor that shows the route of the Green Mountain Railway.

Courtesy of Bethel Historical Society

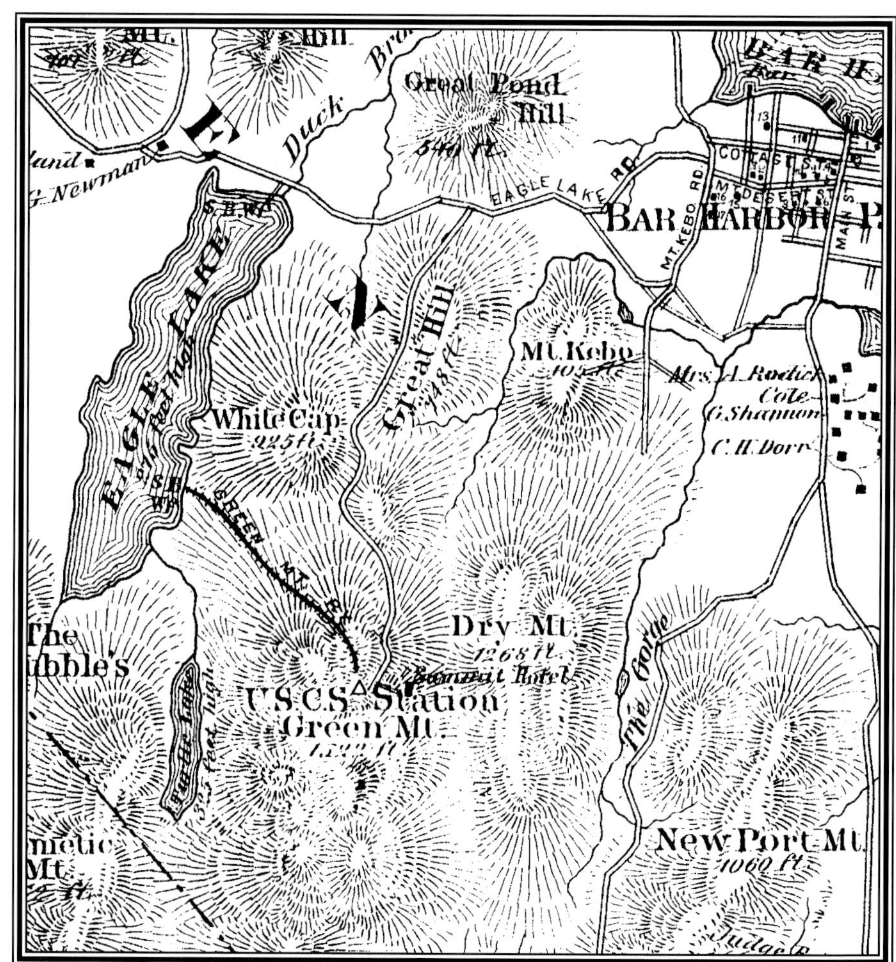

have a locomotive built utilizing the same specifications as recent ones at Mount Washington—and save time and money in the process. One account even claims the locomotive Clergue purchased that spring was originally intended to run on the MWR line.[22]

Among other conditions Maine's 1876 railroad law required Clergue to present "a petition for approval of location" at a public hearing before the state's Board of Railroad Commissioners and publish advance notice of the meeting. Word to that effect appeared in the *Mount Desert Herald* on January 11, 1883, and the hearing took place February 3 in Bangor. The board's three commissioners approved the petition as presented and later in the month accompanied Clergue and GMR's directors to Bar Harbor for a first-hand inspection of the proposed route.

With the go-ahead from the commissioners in hand, Frank Clergue was free to make his plan for a cog railroad a reality. He wasted no time. Initial work commenced February 19, 1883.[23]

Shown in early May 1883, Green Mountain Railway (GMR) locomotive No. 1 pushes a work car toward a construction site a few hundred feet up the mountain, where workers are busy laying track.

Building a Railroad

Railway Construction Begins

Confident his request to build the Green Mountain Railway would receive the necessary state approval, Frank Clergue had placed the following notice in the *Mount Desert Herald's* "Wanted" section for January 18, 1883:

GREEN MOUNTAIN RAILWAY. *Proposals solicited.*

For the whole or any part of the following: Construction of circular stone wall of a house on the summit of Green Mountain, Mount Desert Island, containing about 8000 feet of masonry; carpenter's and painter's work on same.

80 cubic yards of culvert masonry, 6000 cubic yards of earth excavation; 1275 cubic yards of ledge excavation; 700 cubic yards loose rock; drilling of 2000 holes, 6 inches deep. 1 1/2 inches in diameter. 100,000 spruce timber and plank; 2800 railroad ties; clearing and grubbing 6000 feet of track; 6000 feet (superficial) 3-inch plank walk; construction of a wharf on Eagle Lake, about 1000 feet, superficial area.

For transportation of passengers and freight between Bar Harbor and Eagle Lake, in connection with Railway; for transportation of 100 tons railroad material from Bar Harbor to head of Eagle Lake.

> For lease of hotel on summit of Green Mountain, at terminus of Railway.
>
> Right of rejection reserved.

The call for men, materials, and related services was clear and detailed, and several area businesspeople responded. Richard Hamor & Sons, proprietors of Bar Harbor's Grand Central House, gained the bid to clear the proposed route—removing obstructing rocks, roots, and stumps, and smoothing the terrain where practical. The Hamors also supervised transportation of the building materials and the rolling stock from Bar Harbor to the mountain.[1] Off-island crews participated in the overall work, as well. Carpenters and masons from Bangor erected a spacious stone-and-wood hotel on the highest crest of the mountain. Railroad contractor David D. Smith and civil engineer Fred H. Coombs, both from Bangor, furnished the woodwork for the road.[2] Once activity commenced, the engineers and the contractors made their headquarters at the St. Sauveur Hotel in Bar Harbor.[3]

The Railbed

By mid-February enough snow had melted from the mountainside to permit the work of clearing and grubbing to commence. On Monday, February 19, crews began hacking out a nearly 100-foot-wide strip through the forest and dense undergrowth.[4] They worked 12-hour shifts, received daily wages of $1.50, and lived in a temporary boarding house operated by Samuel E. Head at the foot of the railway. During mid-April, 15 laborers struck for higher pay, demanding $1.75 a day.[5] Frank Clergue dismissed the request and the work continued without further incident.

On February 19, 1883, crews began clearing and grubbing a nearly 100-foot-wide strip where the GMR track would be located. Rail laying began the first of May and finished June 22, one day before the railroad's grand opening. Railroad management employed as many as 175 laborers and paid each one $1.50 a day in wages.

Courtesy of Maine Historic Preservation Commission, Augusta

The chosen route mostly spanned stretches where either the ground could be cleared to the underlying rock, or granite ledge was already exposed. Along the way the surface bedrock was uniform enough that very little blasting was necessary to further even it. The steady contour also eliminated the need for trestlework to ensure a relatively constant grade. In a few spots granite crib work carried the track over slight depressions or shallow ravines.[6] In fact, the well-preserved, but overgrown remains of one substantial stone support are still visible roughly halfway up the mountain.[7]

Due to lingering snow and ice the task of preparing the roadbed did not begin in earnest until well into April. Where necessary, workers smoothed the bare rock's irregular face to produce a more consistent incline. While the rock cutting progressed, as many as 15 yoke of oxen began hauling fresh-cut lumber from the green growth near the summit, to use as the foundation for the track.

As soon as the ledge was ready, stone workers drilled laterally parallel rows of holes six inches into the granite and inserted an inch-and-one-quarter iron rod (anchor pin) into each, leaving the exposed ends protruding eight to 12 inches. In series of three the projecting rods formed permanent supports for the foundation logs snugged against them at right angles to the road. Across the logs crews positioned stringers, parallel with the track, and solidly fastened them to both the underlying timbers and the ledge. Next came six-inch, spruce crossties, each secured by two bolts, seven-eighths of an inch in diameter, as well as four spikes and two lagscrews. At sections where a taller foundation was necessary to retain the required grade, crews placed additional alternating tiers of cross-timbers and stringers before anchoring the crossties. A Portland newspaper reporter who visited the railway in June remarked that "the entire structure is as solid as if it were a part of the ledge."[8]

The GMR track measured 6,300 feet in length. It extended from the southeast shore of Eagle Lake, up the western slope of Green Mountain, to a point roughly 300 feet from the actual summit. Along the way the uphill course gained 1,258 feet in elevation.

Courtesy of Maine Historic Preservation Commission, Augusta

The track itself consisted of two conventional T-rails and a central cog rail. On April 2, 90 tons of T-rails, ordered from New York in early February, reached Bar Harbor aboard the 99-foot coasting schooner *Watchman*.[9] The cog rails were assembled at the Atlantic Works in East Boston, where those for the Mount Washington road had been manufactured more than 15 years before.[10]

Rail laying began the first of May and progressed up the mountain as quickly as the foundation structure was in place. During the ensuing seven weeks, crews eventually numbering 140 to 175 pushed the work rapidly. A locomotive and two work cars facilitated moving the heavy rails and other cumbersome construction materials uphill to the current work site.[11] A.S. Randall, an engineer on the Mount Washington Railway the previous 11 years, was hired to drive the locomotive and teach others to operate it in time for GMR's inaugural run.[12]

By May 10, crews had laid 1,200 feet of track.[13] Three weeks later work had progressed halfway up the mountain, prompting supervisors to predict they would have a train at the top by June 23—the day GMR officials originally envisioned as the most suitable for a grand opening.[14] The projection proved accurate. Construction reached the one-mile mark by mid-month, and on June 22, workers hammered the final rail in place.[15]

The Rolling Stock

As work up the western slopes of Green Mountain progressed, Frank Clergue simultaneously moved the multi-faceted project ahead on several fronts. He purchased a 10-ton locomotive from the Manchester (New Hampshire) Locomotive Works, the same firm that had turned out earlier ones for the Mount Washington Railway. He also ordered a passenger car and two work cars from the Hinckley & Egery Iron Company in Bangor.[16]

The Hinckley & Egery Iron Company of Bangor built the construction car and passenger coaches used on the Green Mountain Railway. The completed rigs were transported in sections to Bar Harbor and assembled at the railroad's base station.

Courtesy of Bangor Public Library

The steamship *City of Richmond* began regular passenger and freight service to Mount Desert Island in 1882. The following April the 900-ton sidewheeler was engaged to ferry the recently built GMR locomotive *Mount Desert* from Portland to Bar Harbor. The burly engine proved too large to fit through the steamer's gangway, so railroad officials hired the schooner *Stella Lee* to do the job.

Steamship Historical Society of America, Baltimore, Maryland

Getting the locomotive from Manchester to Eagle Lake proved a real challenge. On April 12 it arrived by rail in Portland and was offloaded for transfer to the Maine Central Railroad steamship *City of Richmond*. The burly engine proved too large for *Richmond's* gangway, so the schooner *Stella Lee* was hired to carry it, reaching Hamor's Wharf in Bar Harbor on Wednesday, April 18. At the dock a moving crew hitched a team of 14 horses to the weighty payload and skidded it up West Street, then south along Bar (now Bridge) Street. Before rounding onto Cottage Street, the movers decided to substitute wheels for runners, to reduce resistance, and added two yoke of oxen for greater pulling power.[17]

Averaging slightly less than one mile a day, the industrious gang of men and animals painstakingly maneuvered the weighty locomotive to the north shore of Eagle Lake, arriving Saturday, April 21. The 2.5-mile journey involved cresting a

The tranquil Bar Harbor waterfront of 1882 bears little resemblance to the frequently bustling one of today. In the center foreground is Hamor's Wharf, where in April 1883, GMR locomotive No. 1 and the steamer *Wauwinet* arrived. During the next few weeks Elihu Hamor employed stout crews and more than a dozen teams of horses to drag the hefty cargoes some two and one-half miles overland, to the north end of Eagle Lake.

Bar Harbor Historical Society

nearly 350-foot rise in elevation, through the gap between Great Pond Hill, the northernmost extent of Green Mountain, and the south side of Great Hill. A large scow purchased by Hamor & Sons also made the trip, to carry workers' tools and equipment and ferry other freight and building materials to the foot of the railway.[18]

The final leg of the passage, a 1.5-mile distance from the north end of Eagle Lake to the railway terminal at the base of the mountain, had to be delayed until enough lake ice could be cut and removed to permit the barge and its unusual cargo to navigate unhindered. On May 3 the *Mount Desert Herald* reported that both the locomotive and a construction car had been landed at the base station, set on temporary rails, and rolled a few hundred feet to a spot opposite the new depot, where workers were putting them in running order. By May 7 both units had been placed on the first section of cog rail.

As its early Mount Washington counterparts, the Green Mountain locomotive, dubbed *Mount Desert*, burned wood and could generate approximately 150 pounds (per square inch) of steam. From the horizontal boiler pressurized vapor was channeled into four independent, double steam cylinders, each pair connected to a separate drive axle. Here the process of converting steam into mechanical energy (and linear motion into rotary motion) occurred, causing the drive axles to turn. As they did, they set in motion a pinion gear and an interlocking axle shaft with its associated spur, ratchet, and cog gears. One tooth after another the slowly revolving cog gear meshed with the rack, set equidistant between the underlying T-rails, and moved the locomotive forward. (The locomotive's traditional wheels simply turned on their axles, instead of being driven.) During the ascent a hinged, pivoting device known as a "pawl" dropped into each successive notch of the revolving ratchet, preventing any backward motion.[19]

The 10-ton locomotive *Mount Desert* burned wood. Its horizontal boiler could generate 150 pounds of steam, which helped drive the diminutive engine up Green Mountain at a carefully controlled speed of slightly more than two miles per hour.

Courtesy of Maine Historic Preservation Commission, Augusta

The open sides of the GMR passenger car permitted riders easy access and allowed panoramic views during the train's ascent and descent. The car contained eight wooden benches, each accommodating six people. The seats were positioned at an angle similar to the grade of the track, which allowed patrons to remain comfortably upright during the trip.

Acadia National Park's William Otis Sawtelle Research and Collections Center, Bar Harbor

The idea of equipping *Mount Desert* with two separate cog wheels was a safety precaution. Should a malfunction occur in any part of the mechanics of one, the likelihood of a disaster would be averted by having the second system continue to operate independently.

Hinckley & Egery workers constructed the passenger car and two work cars in sections, and they were assembled in a workshop within the depot at the foot of the mountain. Unlike the closed coaches at Mount Washington, the Green Mountain passenger car had open sides, providing riders easier access and greater visibility. It held eight wooden benches, each spanning the width of the carriage. One bench could accommodate six people, giving the car a total carrying capacity of 48. The seats, with slatted backs, were positioned at an angle similar to the average grade of the track, so passengers would sit upright during the ride. The benches faced downhill, affording riders expansive views of the surrounding landscape. Roll-up canvas curtains along the sides and ends of the coach could be dropped, to shield travelers from unexpected rain, cold, or strong winds.[20]

The passenger car was fitted with brakes independent of the locomotive. During both the ascent and the descent it remained on the uphill side of the engine and was not coupled to it. If anything unforeseen were to happen to the locomotive, the car's brake could quickly be screwed down, to safely stop and hold the carriage at any point along the route.[21]

The 1.2 miles over which the little train would operate was just short enough that the locomotive could run the entire distance without stopping for water, which was not the case at Mount Washington. There, a holding tank stood alongside the track, slightly more than a mile from the base station, and passing locomotives routinely stopped to refill their boilers.[22]

Wauwinet

Because Bar Harbor village nestles beneath the northeast face of Green Mountain, providing railroad patrons a way to connect with a train running up the remote west side required a bit of creativity—a trait Frank Clergue possessed in abundance. In fact, he had already decided how this would happen. Passengers would take a 20-minute (2.5-mile) carriage ride from intown Bar Harbor to the north end of Eagle Lake, then a 20-minute (1.5-mile) boat cruise down the lake

The GMR depot stood on the southeast shore of Eagle Lake. Arriving passengers reached the remote location via carriage from Bar Harbor to Eagle Lake and a 20-minute cruise aboard the steamer *Wauwinet*.

Courtesy of Maine Historic Preservation Commission, Augusta

The flat-bottomed, former steam-tug *Wauwinet* ferried Green Mountain Railway passengers and freight between the head of Eagle Lake and the railroad's base station.

Mount Desert Island Chamber of Commerce, Mount Desert

to a landing near the train depot. The stage and boat schedules would be coordinated to permit riders convenient access to any of four, daily rail departures to the summit.[23]

In early April Clergue purchased the excursion steamer *Wauwinet*, then quartered at Newburyport, Massachusetts.[24] Meantime, workers were clearing an area 100 by 300 feet at the base of the railway, adjoining the lakeshore, where they would construct a passenger depot, car and engine houses, and a small shed for storing ice. At the shore others began erecting a long wharf where *Wauwinet* would tie up.[25]

Prior to its arrival in Bar Harbor, *Wauwinet* served in various capacities in Massachusetts, including as a tug in Boston Harbor. Built c. 1876 in New Bedford the vessel was taken to Newburyport in 1880, where it underwent a thorough rebuilding, including the installation of a new engine and boiler. In July 1881 the flat-bottomed stern-wheeler was sold to the local Pentucket Navigation Company. During 1882 *Wauwinet* made daily trips along the Merrimac River—from Lawrence to Haverhill, Newburyport, and the ocean.[26]

Wauwinet steamed up to Hamor's Wharf the afternoon of April 17, 1883, one day before the GMR locomotive *Mount Desert* arrived.[27] It lay there until early May, when Elihu Hamor tackled the task of moving the 11.5-ton vessel over the same forested route he had just cajoled the hefty iron-and-steel locomotive.[28] As it turned out, *Wauwinet*'s journey would be even more laborious.

The start of the trip, over relatively flat ground, went reasonably well. By May 9 Hamor's team had hauled the steamer a mile from the starting point, and the *Mount Desert Herald* declared "the movers are making good progress." But the headway slowed as the vessel reached the difficult, uphill portion. During the next week forward movement averaged only a few hundred feet a day.[29] On May 24 *Wauwinet*, a bit worse for the wear, arrived at the north end of Eagle Lake. Workers gave the craft a thorough overhaul before launching it into the chilly lake water. Through mid-June the vessel made numerous working trips, carrying supplies to the base of the railway.[30]

In June, John D. Hopkins, Collector of Customs for the Frenchman Bay District, contacted the U. S. Treasury Department in Washington, informing the agency that Frank Clergue had brought *Wauwinet* to Eagle Lake. Noting that the lake was "entirely disconnected with the ocean or any navigable waters tributary to the ocean," Hopkins wondered whether the steamer should be "registered, enrolled, or licensed." Federal officials replied that since *Wauwinet* was not employed on what were considered "navigable waters of the United States," it would not need to be provided with marine documents. Hopkins was further informed that as long as the vessel remained undocumented, it legally had no home port;

although if it should "get its papers," the home port would be the one nearest the company's established place of business (Bar Harbor), or where the steamer's agent had his business residence (Bangor). *Wauwinet* remained undocumented.[31]

The Green Mountain House

Atop Green Mountain Frank Clergue planned to erect a substantial hotel and dining room for the enjoyment of his patrons, anticipating that many would choose to eat and remain overnight, while savoring the breathtaking views and awe-inspiring sunrises and sunsets during their stays.

On March 1, 1883, GMR directors voted to have work commence at once on the new summit inn, to be called the Green Mountain House.[32] During the month teams of horses hauled building materials—lumber, lime, cement, sand, brick, nails, etc.—up the mountain via the old north ridge carriage road. The first construction began March 29. Workers supervised by N. J. Bunker of Brewer stayed at the top, boarding in Daniel Brewer's 1866 Mountain House.[33] The simple shelter stood only 50 feet from the building site and had been renovated to accommodate them. Progress was rapid, and by the middle of May the wood-frame hotel was complete, except for interior finish work. By then Frank Clergue had announced that Horace W. Chase, who ran the American House in Bangor, had leased the Green Mountain property and would supervise its operation.[34]

The new hotel stood near the apex of Green Mountain's central summit, the highest of three broad peaks roughly 1,000 feet apart. From this spot the surrounding view is the most extensive and takes in the southerly reaches of Mount Desert Island, the Cranberry Isles, Mount Desert Rock, East Penobscot Bay, and a vast sweep of open ocean.

During the spring of 1883, while work progressed laying the track for the Green Mountain Railway, carpentry crews constructed the imposing, three-story Green Mountain House atop the central summit.

Courtesy of Maine Historic Preservation Commission, Augusta

The symmetrical central structure of the Green Mountain House measured 41 by 50 feet. It included two large parlors and a spacious dining room on the first floor, ten sleeping rooms on the second, and ten more on the third. A 26- by 30-foot ell attached to the west end contained six additional bedrooms.

Courtesy of Maine Historic Preservation Commission, Augusta

The main house was symmetrical, situated on an east-west axis. Three stories high, it rested on a 41- by 50-foot granite block foundation. The east end of the first floor contained two large parlors—one for men; the other for women. A spacious dining room, 30 by 41 feet and able to seat 125, filled the west end. An eight-foot veranda, furnished with chairs and settees, surrounded the hip-roofed structure. Four entrances, two on the north side and two on the south, afforded guests direct, convenient access to the dining room and both parlors. A 26- by 30-foot ell, two and one-half-stories high, projected from the west end of the main building. The lower level contained a kitchen, serving room, and pantry.

The hotel's principal staircase led upward from the dining area to the second story, designed with 16 sleeping rooms—10 in the main house and six in the ell. The third story contained 10 more. A separate stairway from the third floor continued up to a sliding scuttle, opening onto a truncated roof and a raised, railed platform. In the center of the platform stood a glass-sided observatory, 10 feet square, topped by a pyramidal spire, 22 feet high at the tip. From it a flagstaff extended the hotel's overall height to 70 feet above the mountaintop.[35]

The original design plans called for additional observation pavilions to be erected on the neighboring eastern and western summits and connected to the hotel by tramways, but with the exception of an observatory built on the eastern peak the following summer, the proposed additional features were never constructed.

Open for Business

By mid-June Frank Clergue had definitely decided to celebrate the Green Mountain Railway's grand opening on Saturday, June 23, and had invited several distinguished guests to partake in the first official trip to the summit. Places aboard

The GMR passenger car was fitted with brakes independent of the locomotive and remained on the uphill side of it. If anything unforeseen were to happen to the engine, the car's brakes could be quickly applied, preventing the carriage from any runaway movement.

Courtesy of Maine Historic Preservation Commission, Augusta

the freshly painted passenger car were reserved for the three Maine railroad commissioners, who would make a final inspection of the entire road; GMR officers and directors; Bangor area dignitaries, including former Vice President Hannibal Hamlin, then living in Hampden; plus a broad contingent of journalists—editors and reporters from major newspapers across New England and beyond. One of the latter fraternity was former war correspondent and renowned political writer George Alfred Townsend of the *Cincinnati Enquirer*. On Thursday, June 21, those making the excursion congregated at the Bangor House for a light evening meal and sociable conversation. At 7:00 the next morning the guests boarded the steamer *Cimbria* and enjoyed a picturesque sail down the Penobscot River, through Eggemoggin Reach, across Blue Hill Bay, and around the southern circuit of Mount Desert Island. Following the docking at Bar Harbor, carriages whisked the entourage to the West End Hotel for a hearty dinner and an overnight stay.

On Saturday morning a convoy of buckboards transported the enthusiastic party to Eagle Lake, where the steamer *Wauwinet* was waiting to carry them to the base station. Shortly after nine a.m., 55 invited guests and railroad personnel crowded onto the little train for the much anticipated ascent. *Eastern Argus* city editor E. S. Osgood described the trip to the top as one made "in perfect smoothness" and "a ride greatly enjoyed by all."[36] When quizzed by a Boston reporter, Hannibal Hamlin remarked, "I feel safer on this road than I do when riding 30 miles an hour on the best surface railroad in the country."[37]

Regular passage on the Green Mountain Railway began the following Saturday, June 30. Patrons had their choice of four trips a day, with stages leaving Bar Harbor at 8:00 and 10:00 a.m. and 2:00 and 4:30 p.m. One-way passage between Bar Harbor and the summit cost $1.75; round trips, $2.50. Intermediate fares were also available for those wanting to experience only certain parts of the route.

*GREEN*MOUNTAIN*RAILWAY*

Stages leave *Bar Harbor* for *Summit* . *9.00* and *11.00* a.m., *2.00* and *4.30* p.m.
Trains leave *Summit* for *Bar Harbor* . *8.50* and *10.50* a.m., *1.50* and *4.20* p.m.

Route of Stages.—From West End Hotel, via Newport, Rockaway, Marlboro, The Rodick, Grand Central, St. Sauveur, Lynam's and Belmont to *Eagle Lake*, there connecting with *Steamer* for *Base Station*, thence by *Mountain Railway* to the *Summit of Green Mountain,*

THE HIGHEST ELEVATION ON THE UNITED STATES COAST.

The view from this point is one of the *finest in the world*, as the thousands who have made the ascent will attest.

The Railway is a *marvel* of engineering skill, and for upwards of 6,000 feet is securely bolted to the solid mountain ledge. *Eagle Lake* is 270 feet above the sea level, and is annually visited by thousands of tourists. *The New Hotel* at the summit is commodious and attractive.

For full information as to rates, special excursions, etc., call at the Company's **Office**, Main Street, Bar Harbor, Me.

In addition to placing ads in area newspapers and posting eye-catching handbills around Bar Harbor, Frank Clergue gave away cards illustrated with images of the Green Mountain Railway train and the steamer *Wauwinet* on one side and a railroad timetable on the other.

The roundabout trip from Bar Harbor to the summit of Green Mountain required passengers take a 20-minute stage ride to the north end of Eagle Lake, before boarding the steamer *Wauwinet* for a 1.5-mile cruise to the railroad's base station. Schedules for the carriage and boat rides were coordinated to meet any of the four waiting trains to the summit. The overall excursion took about 90 minutes.

Acadia National Park's William Otis Sawtelle Research and Collections Center, Bar Harbor

Facing page:

As seen from the base station wharf at Eagle Lake, an ascending Green Mountain Railway train approaches the first of only two curves along the sloping track to the summit. The average rise in elevation along the route was one foot for every 4.5 feet traveled (approximately 22 degrees), while the steepest pitch gained nearly one foot in every three (roughly 30 degrees).

Mount Desert Island Historical Society

In July GMR placed three, 16-passenger "barges" (large, open carriages fitted with lateral seating on both sides) on the Bar Harbor-Eagle Lake run and hired Abner Getchell of Linneus to manage the line. Before leaving town the spacious rigs, custom manufactured in Cambridge, Massachusetts, made the rounds of the local hotels, picking up passengers at the West End, Rockaway, Newport, Marlborough, Rodick, Grand Central, St. Sauveur, Lynam's, and Belmont.

The excursion timetable was carefully coordinated to provide unhurried, yet efficient transport of passengers. *Wauwinet*'s departures from the head of Eagle Lake occurred 45 minutes after barges left Bar Harbor, with trains ascending the mountain 20 minutes after the steamer's sailing. The locomotive required slightly less than 30 minutes to reach the mountaintop, which meant those making the trip from downtown Bar Harbor arrived at the summit in about 90 minutes.[38]

Railroad business the first season was steady and especially busy on Sundays, when a healthy mix of curious Mainers joined the faithful parade of summer visitors. Many who rode the trains stayed overnight at the top. A published list in the August 9, 1883, edition of the *Mount Desert Herald* discloses the names of 177 individuals who had spent at least one night at the summit the previous week. It includes parties from 15 states and one Canadian province.

As the summer wore on, hot weather prevailed and rainfall became increasingly sparse. Into August the woods across the island dried dangerously, and the threat of wildfire became more and more likely. On Tuesday forenoon, August 21, a spark from *Mount Desert*'s stack kindled a fire in the undergrowth some distance from the track, well up on the mountain. Unnoticed at first, it eventually spread into the brush on the north side of the roadbed and quickly burned out of control. Volunteers from the Bar Harbor Fire Department, under the command of foreman E. J. Winship, responded to the blaze, and a gang of firefighters worked

all day and night to at least keep the flames from reaching the summit hotel and the railroad track. The next day a dense layer of smoke settled over Eagle Lake, enveloping *Wauwinet* almost as soon as it left the base station wharf.

Louise de Koven Bowen, a Chicago social reformer and suffragist and an established summer visitor to MDI, was 24 years old that season and rode the GMR train while the wildfire was raging across the mountain. In 1944 she recounted the uncomfortable experience in a small, privately printed volume entitled *Baymeath*, after the elegant summer home she and her banker husband, Joseph T. Bowen, shared at Hulls Cove:

> One summer, before I was married, Jessie Peabody (now Mrs. Herman Butler) and I, and two young men, went up to Green Mountain on a little Funicular railroad. We went over to Eagle Lake in a boat, and then took the railroad up the mountain. When we had almost reached the top, we saw the other side was all afire, and that the wind was blowing the flames around near the railroad. It was a nervous trip up, with the smoke so thick we could hardly see out of the car, but the little engine chugged on, and we finally reached the top.
>
> In those early days there was a little hotel on the top of the mountain, and we four young people had gone up there just to have dinner and spend the day. To our horror, we were told that the train could not go down again through the fire, and that we would have to spend the night up there or else walk down the carriage road, a very old road which was not then used, and it was ablaze. We never even played with the thought of spending the night on the top of the mountain with two young men. It would have been as much as any girl's reputation was worth to have done a thing of that kind. So we decided we would go down the carriage road. The hotel people tried to persuade us not to, saying it was not safe,

Facing page:

The possibility of fire caused by sparks from a GMR locomotive was a constant concern. On August 21, 1883, a passing train ignited a runaway blaze across the upper slopes of Green Mountain. Volunteer crews from Bar Harbor battled the smoky conflagration and kept it from reaching the summit hotel or damaging the ties and foundation timbers along the roadbed.

Courtesy of Randall H. Bennett

Longtime MDI summer resident Louise de Koven Bowen was a passenger on one of the Green Mountain Railway trains during the summer of 1883, while a sizable woods fire was raging nearby. She recounted the unsettling experience in a 1944 book entitled *Baymeath,* the name of her family's magnificent Hulls Cove summer cottage.

Fogler Library Special Collections, University of Maine, Orono

but after eating a bite of luncheon we started down. The going at first was pretty good, and ahead of us the fire had apparently passed the road, but the smoke was intense and the air was red-hot. Our two young men took off their coats, which they put over our heads, and we plunged on down, falling over stones, jumping aside to avoid a blazing branch that had fallen into the road, and trying hard not to step on red-hot ashes which strewed our path. The road was about three miles long. It curved all the time and we could not see what was ahead of us. To go back was impossible, so we went on, hoping for the best. Our feet had some burns on them and the soles of our shoes were almost entirely burned. Our faces smarted from the hot air which struck us, but the greatest part of the fire had crossed the road and we had to make our way through the burning debris. We were glad enough to reach home.

Around six p.m. on the 21st, another fire broke out in the gorge between Dry (Dorr) and Newport (Champlain) mountains and began burning briskly in the dry treetops. Smoke in heavy columns funneled through the gorge, nearly obscuring the surrounding peaks. The same week other fires erupted across the island, including a major conflagration on the Western Mountains in Tremont, where more than 1,500 acres were scorched during a more than two-week stretch. Smaller blazes erupted in the Pretty Marsh area, as did one on Strawberry Hill, immediately south of the intown Bar Harbor business district. Firefighters successfully battled the latter blaze, stopping it before it could cross the Otter Creek Road and endanger the woods on Newport Mountain. Westerly breezes eventually wafted a smoky veil across Frenchman Bay, creating a ghostly pall that persisted for days. On August 23 the *Mount Desert Herald* noted that the Bar Harbor fires posed no immediate danger to any structures, but expressed concern that if the wind should back and strengthen, a "serious time may be expected."[39]

Bangor probate judge and ardent historian John Edward Godfrey visited MDI in mid-September. Writing to his daughter from Southwest Harbor on the 16th, he commented on MDI's extremely dry conditions and rampant fires, as well as his recent trip on the cog railroad:

> The last week has been without a storm. The grass is withered; almost dead; the ground is parched; the fires are running over Green Mountain, and it is a question of time and continued drouth whether they will overrun Mt. Desert Island.
>
> We went up the Green Mountain railway, which was built this year by Bangor capitalists. It is under the superintendence of Capt. Goodwin of Bangor, who is disposed to be polite to us. Mr. Frank Clergue and another man, who are interested in the railway, came here in the *Cimbria* with us. About 150 went up the mountain to-day. The fires bordered the track and the atmosphere was full of smoke, but we had a good view from the summit.[40]

Embattled crews eventually contained the numerous wildfires, although decayed roots and moss on Green Mountain's eastern slopes continued to smolder and smoke well into mid-September.[41] Despite the unusual circumstances GMR trains maintained their regular schedules and even ran occasional extra trips to accommodate passengers with special needs.[42] The initial season concluded Saturday, September 22, with a bargain offer. Those who showed up at the Eagle Lake steamer wharf could purchase round-trip tickets to the summit for one dollar—half the usual fare.[43]

Final figures for 1883 reveal that GMR trains carried 2,697 passengers—a respectable figure considering the initial success of the Mount Washington line, although not necessarily one that met the full expectations of company management and the financial backers.[44] Nevertheless, following a GMR directors' meeting in late October, Frank Clergue painted a bright picture of the corporation's state of affairs, declaring a six percent dividend on the stock of record as of November 1.[45] Despite unexpected heavy expenses incurred fighting fires, GMR showed a net income of $3,135.25, and Clergue announced he would add a second train to the line at the start of the 1884 season.[46] More than that, he was ready to reveal his next ambitious undertaking, one closely associated with the Green Mountain Railway.

CHAPTER FOUR

Another Clergue Scheme

The Mount Desert Railway

At the same time Frank Clergue released news of the Green Mountain Railway's profitable first season, he revealed the essence of another plan—to build a narrow gauge railroad between the GMR terminal, at the foot of Green Mountain, and Bar Harbor village. The new enterprise would be called the Mount Desert Railway (MDR) and do business under basically the same ownership and management as the Green Mountain Railway.

In characteristic fashion, Clergue had begun implementing the new scheme prior to talking about it publicly. Before word of the proposal appeared in the Bangor and Bar Harbor papers, he dispatched Bangor engineer Fred Danforth to survey the proposed route. He also arranged for a preliminary hearing before the Board of Railroad Commissioners. It would take place Friday evening, November 2, 1883, at the Penobscot Exchange Hotel in Bangor.

Although the eleventh-hour public notice gave the railroad's adversaries short notice, they worked swiftly to organize their opposition and hired Ellsworth

Following the Green Mountain Railway's profitable first season, Frank Clergue announced he wanted to build a narrow gauge railroad from the station at the foot of Green Mountain to intown Bar Harbor. The plan immediately drew strong, persistent criticism from a broad range of island residents and summer cottagers.

Sault Ste. Marie (Ontario) Public Library

attorneys Andrew Peters Wiswell and Hannibal E. Hamlin—the latter, the son of the former Vice President—to represent them. The day before the forum the *Mount Desert Herald* provided a measure of editorial support, calling the plan "a project which needs very careful consideration." The piece went on to state:

> Our summer residents come here to be rid of the noise, smoke, and dust of railroads, and both they and our permanent residents are very generally of the opinion that Lamoine Point or Hancock Falls is near enough for railroads of either broad or narrow gauge. We understand that a strong remonstrance to the building of any more railroads in this vicinity will be presented to the railroad commissioners at the hearing tomorrow evening.

At the hearing Frank Clergue presented his petition, whereupon Wiswell and Hamlin proceeded to make a vigorous case against it. During the latter's remarks the railroad commissioners reminded the two attorneys this was only an introductory meeting, and while they could verbally state their objections, it was neither the time nor the place to present the lengthy, written remonstrance they were prepared to introduce. They would have that chance at a formal hearing, slated for Bar Harbor on November 30.

On the eve of the Bar Harbor gathering the *Herald* took a strong editorial stand against what it called "That Proposed Railroad," insisting that the island's resident and non-resident property holders—and the summer visitors, as well— were all unanimously opposing it. The paper concluded its remarks by urging the commissioners to reject the plan: "When everything is against a thing and nothing for it, it is hard to conceive how any aid or comfort can be extended to it by any law-giving body in the State."

The formal hearing was held in the village schoolhouse, where Frank Clergue addressed an overflow crowd almost entirely against the new undertaking. In his extended remarks Clergue indicated that his company had originally intended to lay a track between Eagle Lake and the steamboat wharf, including a lengthy stretch of Bar Harbor shorefront. But he had since learned of the strong objections to that idea and consequently amended the formal petition to have it end the line at "some spot on Eden Street, near James Eddy's store." This would have placed the terminus near today's junction of West and Eden streets. Although the audience listened in polite silence, Clergue's remarks did nothing to change their dissatisfaction with the scheme and, if anything, solidified their resolve to kill its prospects as quickly and forcefully as possible.

Once Clergue finished speaking he left the meeting, and a trio of area residents rose in turn to express contrary points of view. Fountain Rodick, one of the family operating the cavernous, six-story Rodick House on Main Street, was the first to speak. He began by saying the Green Mountain Railway had been "forced upon the people of the island" before they had the chance to voice their opinions of it. He cautioned that the Mount Desert Railway would have appeared in the same fashion, if it weren't for the fact that a few alert individuals had seen the public notice shortly before the initial hearing. He went on to remind everyone that Clergue's MDR petition included other provisions, including the right to operate steamships on the navigable waters of the State of Maine and erect hotels and restaurants in connection with them. He maintained that approval of the plan would open the door to creating a monopoly of the area's points of interest for the benefit of single individuals or corporations. Rodick concluded by saying that visitors came to the island "for relief from the hurry and bustle of the busy world,"

Facing page (left):

Ellsworth native Andrew Peters Wiswell fashioned a distinguished career as a trial lawyer, bank president, and magistrate. In 1900 he became the youngest individual ever appointed Maine chief justice. As senior member of the Ellsworth law firm Wiswell, King, and Peters, he represented a group of MDI summer residents trying to prevent Frank Clergue from establishing the Mount Desert Railway, a narrow gauge road that would initially link the Green Mountain line with intown Bar Harbor and eventually extend to other towns across the island.

Courtesy of Union Trust Company, Ellsworth

and the buckboard and carriage were swift enough modes of transportation for them.

Dr. R. L. Grindle of neighboring Somesville followed Rodick to the podium and assured everyone that those in his community and the others across the island were as opposed to a railroad on MDI as the people in Bar Harbor. He asserted:

> When visitors first came to this island they objected to the well water. Did we immediately fetch in chemists with their microscopes to analyze the well water and try to prove to the visitors that it was for their benefit to drink well water? No, we set to work and supplied them with lake water. If the people who come here want a thing and it is for our interests to supply it, let them have it. If they don't want a certain thing, and in this case it is very apparent they don't want a railroad, then do all you can to prevent it; the people in Mount Desert and all over the island will support you.

After Grindle, Rev. C. S. Leffingwell stepped up to declare that he heartily endorsed all Mr. Rodick and Dr. Grindle had said and could only add that the proposed railroad was "in entire opposition to the interests of the island as a summer resort."

After the discussion concluded, the commissioners scheduled a follow-up meeting for Wednesday, January 16, 1884, when they intended to decide the railroad's fate. During the intervening weeks the *Herald* continued to publish opinions and viewpoints against the venture. A few appeared as editorials, but most were expressed in letters from unnamed readers identified only by such pseudonyms as: "A Summer Resident of Bar Harbor," "A Property Owner and Summer Resident of Mount Desert," and "Resident." Among the remarks the anonymous writers called the plan "objectionable," an "outrage," and "a serious

Near left:
During the heated Mount Desert Railway proceeding, Andrew Wiswell collaborated with another Ellsworth notable, attorney Hannibal E. Hamlin, son of Vice President Hannibal Hamlin, who served under Abraham Lincoln. The younger Hamlin later joined the political ranks, becoming President of the Maine Senate (1901–1902) and Maine Attorney General (1905–1908).

Courtesy of Hale & Hamlin, Ellsworth

drawback" to the islanders' comfort and the value of their property. One warned that "a screaming, smoking locomotive, crossing the streets and neighborhood drives, frightening horses with their whistles and burning up the wood—one of the great charms of Mount Desert—from their sparks" would be a serious injustice "to the great majority of the persons who seek their summer rest and recreation" on the island.

Railroad commissioners D. N. Mortland (chair), John F. Anderson, and A. W. Wildes convened the emotion-charged January hearing shortly before five p.m.

in the music room at the St. Sauveur. After opening remarks those present decided the chamber where they were gathered was too cold for comfort and agreed to adjourn until 7:00 p.m., when they would resume the proceedings at the nearby District Hall. During the evening both sides paraded several speakers on their behalf, each offering mostly the same arguments as at the earlier meeting. Frank Clergue took the floor first, then yielded to MDR superintendent Fred Danforth and company director Franklin Cram. Attorneys Hamlin and Wiswell led the charge for the remonstrants, cross-examining each of the petitioners before calling on Fountain Rodick to again speak for the townspeople and the summer visitors.

At 11:00 p.m. the spirited session was still in progress, prompting the commissioners to adjourn for the night and reconvene the following morning, when each side would be given one hour for closing arguments. Shortly before noontime on the 17th Chairman Mortland declared the hearing concluded. He then announced that the matter required additional consideration, and he and his colleagues would not render a decision that day. As it turned out, more than two weeks passed before the official word was handed down.

The commission's ruling, rendered February 1, proved a bittersweet victory for both sides. Frank Clergue would be allowed to build his railroad, but only between the base of Green Mountain and the outskirts of Bar Harbor. Those in Bar Harbor village would not have to put up with the noise or distraction of a shore-front railroad, but neither they nor the other objectors could prevent Clergue and his associates from going ahead with the new line.

The final decree was lengthy and referred back to the inception of the Green Mountain Railway as the grounds for the commissioners' findings. Based on the number of passengers carried by GMR trains the previous summer, the committee recognized it as a legitimate public conveyance, according to Maine law. In so doing it justified the proposed Mount Desert Railway as a rightful "branch" of the Green Mountain line. The board also deemed much of the testimony of the remonstrants as speculative, "as from the nature of the case it could not be otherwise." In its words:

> Nature has given to Mount Desert Island some of the grandest scenery on the globe. It was placed there not for the eye of the rich, but for the public; for those who stay but a day as well as those who stay months and years; and for the purpose of viewing it they may avail themselves of the more modern means of travel, whether the object be business or pleasure. And we think railroads may be lawfully constructed to meet the demands of the public in this respect, and that the right of eminent domain may be exercised for such purpose.

The heart of the decision was contained in the following statements:

> . . . our finding is that the public convenience and exigencies require such a railroad as the petitioners propose to construct.
>
> But we think that the objection of the remonstrants . . . is well founded. While it would undoubtedly be convenient for this corporation to have the road constructed to a point to connect with steamboats to and from that place, we do not think the public exigencies demand it . . . Bar Harbor village is not a commercial centre, but a place of summer resort, the home, for the time being, of the public who resort there, and they have an interest in it, as such, with all its varied attractions, which ought not needlessly to be broken in upon and destroyed, or greatly injured, as it undoubtedly would, by running a railroad along the shore front through the village.

> We are also convinced that the construction and operation of such road through that village as proposed, would in effect . . . destroy the value of residential and real estate in that locality, and of estates in its immediate vicinity. We therefore do not approve so much of the location of said road . . . and the prayer of the petitioners, in that respect, must be denied.[1]

The compromise did little to resolve the bitter debate. That summer another element of the railroad's opponents, wishing to make their position perfectly clear, went on record with its feelings. On August 21, 1884, between 300 and 400 non-resident property holders and summer visitors gathered at the St. Sauveur. Among the several who spoke, Samuel E. Lyon read a prepared resolution containing a synopsis of the various arguments put forward by those who opposed Clergue's intentions. In its words:

> *First:* Establishment of the Mount Desert Railway would not be a profitable investment, considering the cost of land required to be taken, construction of equipment for the road, and compensation for likely damage by fire to the surrounding forests;
>
> *Second:* The distance from the steamboat landing and the town's principal hotels would first require transporting passengers by coach between the various points; and since the current trip to Eagle Lakes takes but 40 minutes, it is unlikely that any appreciable time would be saved via the new system;
>
> *Third:* The operation of a steam train is too noisy, and its crossing of public roads and drives would be objectionable to a great many persons seeking rest and quiet during the summer season; and

Fourth: The railroad's proposed route passes through extensive valuable woodlands. Based on the number of fires caused by Green Mountain Railway trains in 1883, it is logical to expect MDR's locomotives will also jeopardize the forests along its road.

Those present wholeheartedly agreed with the points and voted that a copy of them be sent to the officers of the Mount Desert Railway, as well as to Payson Tucker, general manager of the Maine Central Railroad.[2]

In the end it would be the anti-railroad coalition that ultimately won the day. Realizing he would be challenged every step of the way and suffer additional ill will in the process, Frank Clergue postponed building the Mount Desert Railway that year. Although he kept the project legally alive until 1892, it never materialized.[3]

After the close of the Green Mountain Railway's 1883 season, Frank Clergue felt sufficiently encouraged that he ordered a second locomotive and another passenger car, each identical to its predecessor. The newer locomotive was simply called "No. 2," without any further designation. Clergue had this "posed" view taken to showcase the new train.

Bar Harbor Historical Society

CHAPTER FIVE

GMR: Successive Seasons

1884: Improvements and Setbacks

Preparations for the Green Mountain Railway's 1884 season got underway well before regular summer service was scheduled to begin. Frank Clergue arrived in Bar Harbor in early May, to ensure that last-minute details would be dealt with in plenty of time.[1] The previous winter he had pursued the matter of adding a second train to the line and purchased (from the firms that built the previous ones) another locomotive and an additional passenger car—both identical to their predecessors.

Clergue also authorized and initiated improvements and enhancements to existing facilities. At Eagle Lake a work crew enlarged the steamboat wharf, while another repainted and refitted *Wauwinet*.[2] On Green Mountain's eastern summit, carpenters began putting up a 75-foot, octagonal observatory, where visitors could enjoy bird's-eye views of Bar Harbor village, the Porcupine Islands, Frenchman Bay, and the northeastern extent of Mount Desert Island. During early June the railroad commissioners came to town, inspected the track and all rolling stock, and found the line in "a perfectly safe condition."[3]

Shown at the base station in the spring of 1884, the second GMR train (left) has recently arrived. The new passenger car awaits installation of seats and roll-up curtains, which shielded riders in the event of rain, cold, or strong winds.

Mount Desert Island Historical Society

Locomotive No. 2 sits atop Green Mountain. The debarkation point for passengers arriving at the top was a narrow platform some 100 yards west of the central summit, the highest of three broad peaks situated approximately 1,000 feet apart.

Courtesy of Maine Historic Preservation Commission, Augusta

The new season kicked off with relatively little fanfare. Beginning June 23 management advertised on-demand trains for parties of 10 or more and on Monday, July 7, resumed four scheduled, daily trips, as had been offered the previous season.[4] Early reports suggested that business was good, and company expectation ran high it would continue that way. Then, in early August, an unforeseen disaster occurred atop Green Mountain.

Fire Destroys the Green Mountain House

Shortly after sunset, Saturday evening, August 2, 1884, several Bar Harbor towns-people noticed a bright orange glow behind the eastern peak of Green Mountain. Some speculated that a forest fire had broken out in the woods on the back side of the summit. Others thought perhaps overnight partygoers had kindled a huge bon-fire somewhere near the top. A few even suggested the year-old Green Mountain House was ablaze. Shortly after 8:30 p.m. a phone call to the *Mount Desert Herald* offices settled the issue. A caller from Otter Creek, where the summit buildings were plainly visible, confirmed the big hotel was not only afire, but already mostly consumed. Furthermore, the nearby Mountain House had ignited and was also fully involved.[5]

The fire had broken out on the roof of the main house, apparently started by sparks flying from the kitchen chimney. An eight-year-old girl staying in the hotel with her mother and sister happened to look out a window and noticed what she described as a "sheet of flame." The mother quickly whisked the child outside to a place of safety, then returned to the smoke-filled interior to retrieve their possessions.[6] But the flames were spreading so rapidly she could neither find nor save much of anything. With no firefighting equipment or water at their disposal, the token hotel staff were helpless to stop the raging inferno, and both summit structures quickly burned to their foundations, leaving only the shafts of two brick chimneys rising starkly from a mass of gray ash.

During the evening a man living on the west side of Eagle Lake spotted the flames. He rowed across to the railroad's base station and awakened one of the engineers, who ran a train to the summit and brought down the few stranded guests and employees.

The evening of August 2, 1884, fire broke out on the main roof of the Green Mountain House. Hotel staff and guests escaped the rapidly spreading flames, but were helpless to stop the soon-raging inferno. In a matter of minutes the fire leveled the once-proud structure, together with the old Mountain House, which stood about 50 feet west of the hotel.

Courtesy of Maine Historic Preservation Commission, Augusta

The Green Mountain House had been leased to Horace W. Chase of Bangor, who estimated his loss at $4,000. He had insured the business for $1,500. GMR had spent about $8,000 to have the hotel built and carried a $5,500 policy against its destruction.[7]

A Temporary Structure Erected

Undeterred by the calamity, GMR directors took immediate measures to put up a temporary replacement for the former Green Mountain House. Within 48 hours management had gotten plans drawn for a new structure; contracted with Bar Harbor builder John E. Clark to erect it; hired construction workers; ordered the necessary building materials, including 10,000 feet of lumber, in Bar Harbor and Ellsworth; and had them transported by rail, ferry, and horse to Eagle Lake, where they awaited transport to the mountaintop.

Work began August 5 on the stopgap building, which company officials had decided should stand on the eastern summit, adjoining the recently constructed observatory. Once the two-story framework was up, carpenters modified the observatory stairway to allow access between it and the guest house's second floor. The finished structure measured 35 by 45 feet. The lower level included a 21- by 34-foot dining room, a 12- by 17-foot parlor, and a 20- by 30-foot office. The upper floor was divided into eight bedrooms. By August 15 the urgently completed accommodation had opened for business, and innkeeper Chase was serving what the *Mount Desert Herald* termed "most appetizing" meals in a dining area swelled with exuberant, appreciative guests.[8]

GMR's 1884 season concluded Saturday, September 21. The following day a single train made a special run for the enjoyment of company officials and their guests. Management had reason to be pleased—and optimistic. Revenue was up significantly from the previous year; more than 5,000 people had paid to take the mountain excursion.[9] Eager to see a full return to normal operations, GMR directors met a week later and voted to replace the former Green Mountain House with an even more splendid facility, located where the temporary one stood.[10]

The Summit House

During February 1885 management contracted with John Clark to erect a new, full-service hotel—to be called the Summit House. Wanting to get an early start on construction, Clark planned to skid the building materials across the ice on Eagle Lake to the foot of the railway, where the cog train would carry them to the top. But once he learned it would be April before the locomotives could run, he decided to employ several teams of horses to cart equipment and supplies up the timeworn carriage road. Begun in early March, the strenuous undertaking took nearly three weeks.[11]

Using plans drawn by W. E. Mansur of Bangor, Clark had crews at work on the summit in early April. The general design called for an enlargement of the temporary quarters erected the previous summer, which GMR people concluded were too valuable to be taken down. It added a 35- by 40-foot extension to the north end of the existing building and made the entire structure three stories high, capping it with a slate roof. A veranda surrounded the entire first floor, which had been configured to include an office, parlor, dining hall, private dining space, kitchen, and pantry. The second and third levels each contained 10 sleeping rooms with shared baths. Open fireplaces in the dining hall, parlor, and hallways provided warmth and added to the charm. A basement area gave space

Railroad management worked quickly to replace the incinerated Green Mountain House with a smaller, temporary building. Between the 1884 and 1885 seasons they had the makeshift quarters enlarged into the three-story edifice shown in this architectural rendering. The original (1884) structure includes the bottom two stories to the right of the octagonal observatory.

Acadia National Park's William Otis Sawtelle Research and Collections Center, Bar Harbor

for a 30,000-gallon cement cistern and a series of storerooms. Clark's workers finished the job in mid-June, comfortably ahead of the planned July 1 opening. The entire project cost approximately $5,000.[12]

Railway Business Declines

Succeeding seasons through the 1880s saw the Green Mountain Railway Company continue efforts to improve the quality of its operation by further enhancing the

This bird's-eye view of Bar Harbor, published in 1886, includes the sloping profile of Green Mountain, with the recently completed Summit House and a smoke-belching cog train approaching the top.

Acadia National Park's William Otis Sawtelle Research and Collections Center, Bar Harbor

The image of a Green Mountain Railway train as the centerpiece of an 1886 Mount Desert guidebook cover lent further credibility to the railroad's claim of being the area's foremost tourist attraction. Note that the artist mistakenly pictured the locomotive uphill from the passenger car. For patrons' greater safety it always operated on the downhill side.

Courtesy of Maine Historic Preservation Commission, Augusta

level of service it offered. To bolster early season business, trains were made available on demand throughout June, rather than simply the latter part of the month. As the 1885 season got underway, management announced additional stage service connecting Bar Harbor with Eagle Lake. Barges would continue making the customary stops at intown hotels and also call at private cottages for parties of five or more.[13] The following year two more stages were added to the line, making a total of five.[14] During 1889 the cog trains made an additional two trips a day, with the earliest and latest runs reserved for people staying at the Summit House.[15] That season crews laid numerous replacement cross-ties and stringers along the roadbed, as added precaution to ensure the safety of the train and its passengers.[16]

The 1886 season proved to be the most successful, when close to 8,000 people rode the trains.[17] During early July the line benefited greatly from an added influx of summer visitors, as Bar Harbor played host to a conference of the American Institute of Instruction, the oldest educational association in the United States.[18] Between 1,000 and 1,500 faculty and administrators from school systems across the northeast attended the four-day convention, and most took time to enjoy an outing on the Green Mountain Railway.[19]

Despite the attempts to further boost business, GMR ridership declined dramatically after 1886. During 1887 the (estimated) final tally fell to little more than 2,500.[20] In 1888, a poor summer, weather-wise, the number dropped to just 990[21] and was only marginally better—a total of 1,305—the following season.[22] Several writers have suggested that lean years in the local tourist business, marked by changing attitudes and habits among summer visitors, were largely the reason for the downturn.[23] While these may have contributed to the overall result, the major factor was the establishment of a new means of travel to the mountaintop—a much improved roadway up Green Mountain's north ridge.

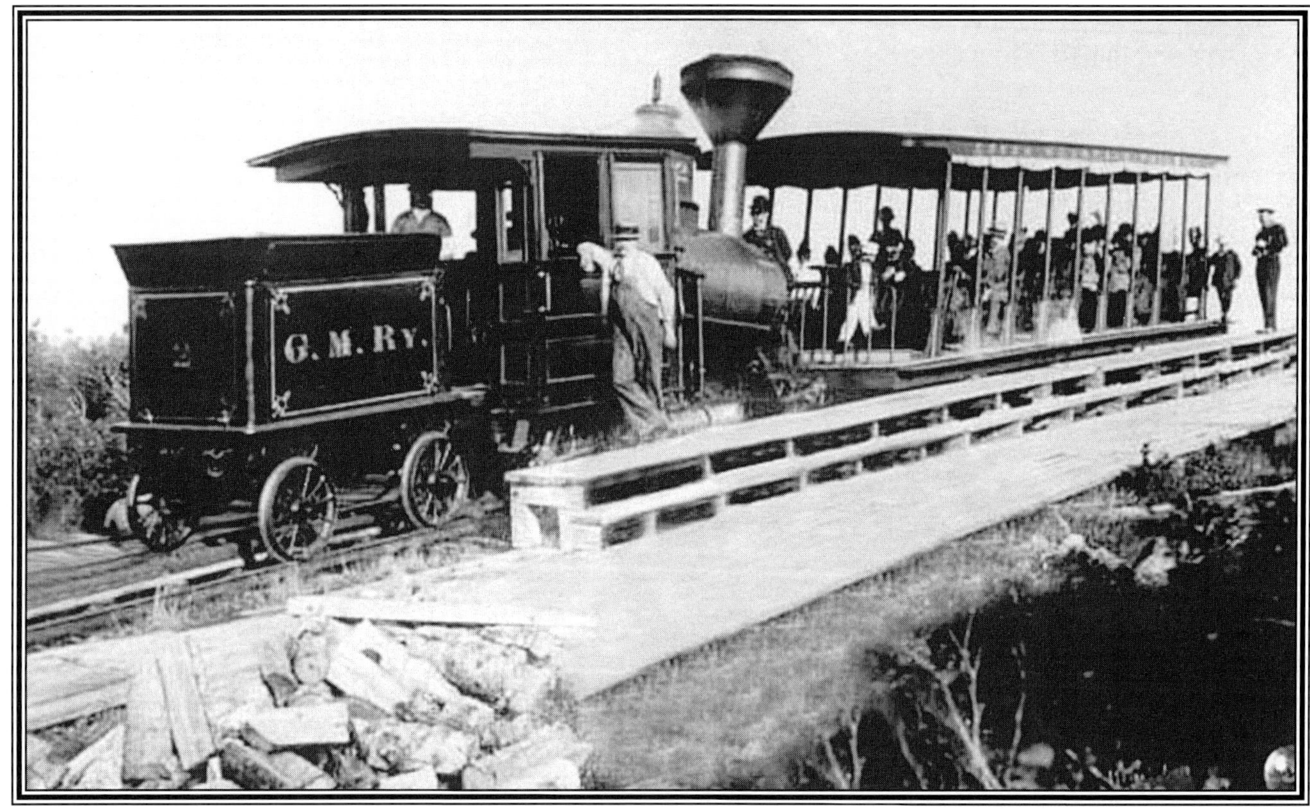

Locomotive No. 2 waits at the summit for downbound passengers. Travel on the Green Mountain Railway reached its height during the summer of 1886, when nearly 8,000 people rode the trains.

Acadia National Park's William Otis Sawtelle Research and Collections Center, Bar Harbor

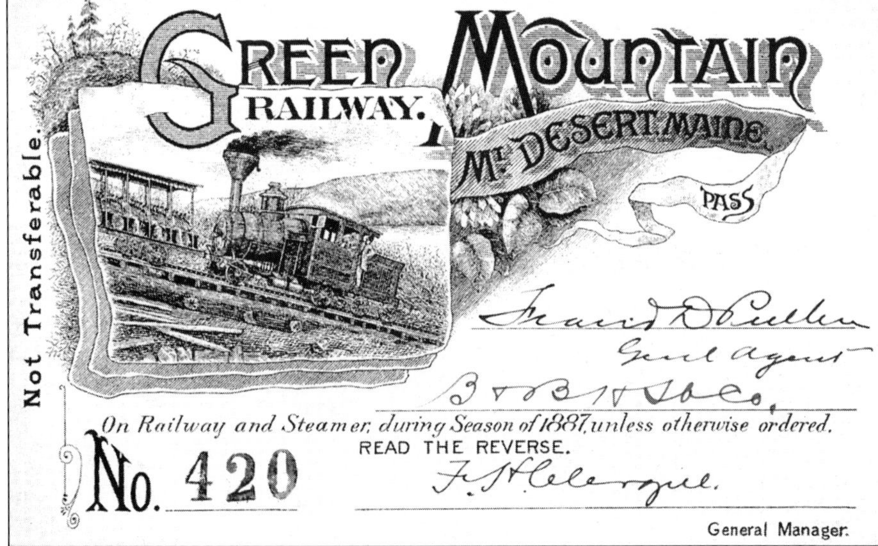

Top:

The Green Mountain Railway provided free transportation to many VIPs, especially if railroad brass thought the courtesy rides would in any way enhance business. This 1887 season pass, given to Frank D. Pullen, General Agent for the Bangor & Bar Harbor Steamship Company, is signed "Francis H. Clergue" and allowed Pullen complimentary travel aboard the steamer *Wauwinet* and any of the GMR trains.

Bottom:

A Green Mountain Railway ticket dated September 3, 1888.

Acadia National Park's William Otis Sawtelle Research and Collections Center, Bar Harbor

The endeavor was the result of a joint effort by local businesspeople calling them-selves the Green Mountain Carriage Road Company.

The Green Mountain Carriage Road Company

Shortly before the Green Mountain Railway's grand opening in 1883, company officials had mildly hinted they would interrupt travel on the existing carriage road by putting up a gate where it crossed the track, slightly above the 1,400-foot level.[24] The warning was never carried out, as much as anything because the old dirt-and-stone thoroughfare was in such poor shape. Erosion had all but eradicated some sections, making it nearly impossible for horses and buckboards to navigate without major difficulty. At the more challenging stretches, riders had to get out and walk, so drivers could coax teams and empty rigs along.[25] Aside from the car-riage road's rundown condition, railroad management was optimistic that once its trains began running, people would flock to them almost exclusively.

For five seasons the Green Mountain Railway provided the only established transportation to the summit of Green Mountain. In late 1887 the prospect of meaningful competition unexpectedly emerged. That December Bar Harbor mer-chants Elihu and Ralph Hamor, with dry goods dealer John J. Carr, organized the Green Mountain Carriage Road Company (CRC) and raised $25,000 to "pur-chase, lease, and acquire land from the base of Green Mountain to the summit, on which to locate, construct, and operate a toll road."[26]

The plan called for work on the ambitious project to begin the following spring, although the start-up was postponed after the task of acquiring a right-of-way up the mountain became more time-consuming than the organizers antici-pated. Once it did begin, in early July, Joseph G. Kelly of Bar Harbor oversaw the

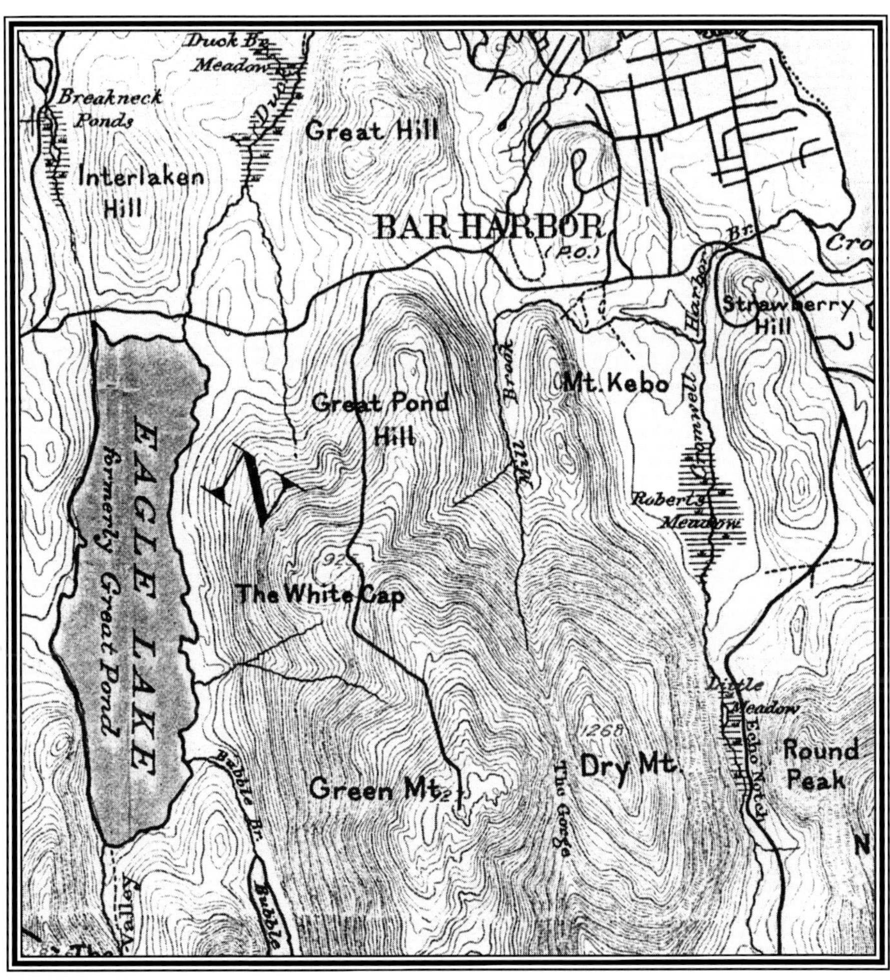

Naturalists Edward Lothrop Rand and John Howard Redfield published this 1894 map, which shows the route of the recently constructed Green Mountain Carriage Road. Beginning at the top of the notch between Great Hill and Great Pond Hill, west of intown Bar Harbor, the roadway climbed south from the Eagle Lake Road, closely following the north ridge of the mountain.

Courtesy of Bangor Public Library

A major reason for the serious decline in ridership on the Green Mountain Railway was the opening of the Green Mountain Carriage Road in July 1888. Conceived by a trio of Bar Harbor businessmen, the 2.5-mile route was constructed at a cost of some $8,000. This ad for the road appeared in July issues of the *Bar Harbor Record*, a popular weekly newspaper of the day.

Jesup Library, Bar Harbor

Green Mountain Carriage Road.

COMPLIMENTARY TICKET.

M ___ _J. W. Somes & Sadie_ ___

NOT TRANSFERABLE.

GOOD FOR SEASON OF 1888.

Patrons of the Green Mountain Carriage Road paid a toll of ten cents, which was collected at a small booth at the entrance to the roadway. Complimentary tickets were issued during 1888, including this one to "Mr. J. W. Somes & Sadie."

Mount Desert Island Historical Society, Mount Desert

construction. Under his direction workers made non-stop progress and completed the job in only three weeks. The lower portion of the route lay slightly to the east of the older road, where it more quickly gained the crown of the mountain's north ridge and provided superior views. The upper section essentially followed the course of the previous approach. The entire way, from the Eagle Lake Road to the summit, measured slightly more than 2.5 miles and was wide enough for two carriages to easily meet and pass one another.[27]

Completed at a cost of $8,000, the Green Mountain Carriage Road opened July 26, 1888.[28] Edwin A. Atlee of Philadelphia was the first to make the scenic drive to the top.[29] The road stayed open until October 1 and attracted more than 3,000 people.[30]

Local livery operators were quick to take advantage of the new Green Mountain Carriage Road by offering buckboard rides from Bar Harbor to the summit. These ads, promoting the services of Andrew Stafford (left) and A. S. Getchell (right), appeared in Bar Harbor newspapers during the summer of 1889.

Jesup Library, Bar Harbor

Open Hostility

Encouraged by the immediate success of the new venture, Carr and the Hamors hired crews to repair and grade the CRC roadbed the following spring, then reopened it June 17, nearly three weeks before the Green Mountain Railway ran its first scheduled train.[31] That day—July 6, 1889—carriage road travelers encountered an unexpected surprise shortly before they reached the mountaintop. Railroad employees had placed a gate across the road where the track crossed it.

Claiming the right of possession to the land at and around the summit, GMR management had employed an attendant to charge passers-by a dollar per person, plus a dollar per vehicle to proceed. The ploy was short-lived; the next morning angry CRC people tore down the barrier.[32]

Tensions between GMR and CRC persisted, then resurfaced later in the month. The night of July 23, six anonymous "railroad people" rode the cog train to the top of the mountain, walked part way down the carriage road, dug a hole, planted dynamite, and blew up a portion of the roadway. CRC supporters immediately talked retaliation, threatening a lawsuit and the possibility someone might dynamite the GMR track.[33] Cooler heads eventually prevailed, and the momentary "road war" ended without further disruption or damage to either company's holdings. Nevertheless, newspaper ads for the railroad later in the season continued to advise that passengers and teams ascending the carriage road would be charged $1.00 per head to enter the summit grounds.[34]

The carriage road's triumphant revival spawned a new wave of entrepreneur, each eager to provide would-be mountain visitors the opportunity for easier, faster ways to visit Green Mountain's summit. The day the improved carriage road opened, Andrew Stafford began operating excursions to the top via a "very stylish" buckboard, built especially for the demanding ride by Ellsworth carriage maker Henry E. Davis. Leaving at 9:30 a.m. and 2:30 p.m. from his stable on Spring Street in Bar Harbor, Stafford and a three-horse hitch made the circuit of intown hotels to pick up passengers. He promised that those who made the morning trip would be back in time for lunch, while ones who went in the afternoon would not miss their "early tea."[35] A. S. Getchell, the proprietor of the Green Mountain Livery, offered on-demand service, advertising a variety of carriages and drivers "at short notice."[36]

After the Green Mountain Carriage Road opened in 1888, Ellsworth carriage maker Henry E. Davis custom-designed a heavy-duty, commercial buckboard especially suited for the demanding trip up and down Green Mountain.

Jesup Library, Bar Harbor

In 1889 the U.S. Signal Service opened a seasonal weather station at the summit of Green Mountain, with offices located on the third floor of the Summit House. At the right is the louvered, wooden shelter that housed instruments for measuring temperature, relative humidity, and atmospheric pressure.

Bar Harbor Historical Society

U.S. Signal Station

The year 1889 brought a new and different activity to the summit of Green Mountain. That summer the Summit House became the site of a first-class "signal station," where trained War Department observers made periodic daily readings of local weather conditions. Talk of such a facility at Bar Harbor dated back to 1883,[37] although internal strife within the U.S. Signal Service delayed the establishment several years.[38]

In October 1888 General Adolphus W. Greely, renowned polar explorer and the service's Chief Signal Officer, visited Bar Harbor to explore the feasibility and logistics of placing a seasonal station atop Green Mountain.[39] The following

Despite a sharp decrease in business after 1886, Green Mountain Railway officials continued to advertise as always, while further enhancing existing services and making improvements and upgrades to the line.

Jesup Library, Bar Harbor

—THE—
Green Mountain Railway

Will continue to be the chief attraction at Bar Harbor. Green Mountain is the highest elevation on the United States coast, the view being one of the finest in the world, as thousands who have made the ascent will attest. The railway is a marvel of engineering skill, and for upwards of six thousand feet is sucurely bolted to the solid mountain ledge. Eagle Lake is 275 feet above the sea-level and is annually visited by thousands of tourists.

THE SUMMIT HOUSE

Is commodious and attractive, has accommodations for 100 guests, with all modern improvements. The Cuisine is unsurpassed, and the the table is supplied with all marketable delecacies in their season. Four trains daily to and from Bar Harbor. Address

GREEN MOUNTAIN RAILWAY.

1137   Bangor, Me.

March Corporal Edward P. Jones, formerly in charge of the signal station in Portland, traveled to Bar Harbor to superintend the task of setting up and conducting a similar operation at Green Mountain.[40] In May, Jones announced he had arranged with GMR officials to place an observatory on the roof of the Summit House and utilize two third-floor rooms (Nos. 18 and 19) as office space.[41] Fitted with the latest meteorological instruments, telegraphy gear, and a telephone, the second-order Green Mountain Signal Station officially opened July 9, 1889.[42] Corporal Jones systematically recorded readings of temperature, relative humidity, atmospheric pressure, wind speed and direction, sky conditions, and precipitation, transmitting data to the agency's central office in Washington. The station closed for the season September 10[43] and reopened the following July, this time in charge of Robert M. Hardinge, who left a similar post in Little Rock, Arkansas, to come to Bar Harbor.[44] Hardinge's stay would likewise be brief. S. G. Duffey replaced him the next summer. The observatory, by this time the responsibility of the U.S. Department of Agriculture, permanently ceased operations at midnight, August 31, 1891.[45]

Out of Business

Following GMR's woeful 1888 and 1889 seasons, management tried desperately to come up with ways to revive interest in the railroad. In early May 1890 the company announced it had reduced the round-trip train fare from $2.50 to $1.00.[46] The idea did bring substantially more business. Nearly every day during August, extra buckboards had to be used to carry passengers to and from Eagle Lake.[47] But the operating season was short, lasting only from mid-July to mid-September, and revenue from the more than 2,300 cheaper fares was not nearly enough to offset

In an attempt to better compete for patrons after the opening of the Green Mountain Carriage Road, railroad officials added more buckboards to the Eagle Lake run and, in 1890, reduced the round-trip train fare from $2.50 to $1.00. The inducements did bring substantially more customers, but not nearly enough to offset mounting debts, which eventually totaled more than $14,000.

Courtesy of Maine Historic Preservation Commission, Augusta

expenses.[48] The line lost $1,400 that season, and the company's already substantial deficit, dating back to 1887, increased to $14,049.57.[49] Seeing no way to reverse the growing financial plight, GMR directors shut down the railroad.

The end came quietly and received little attention in the local papers. A brief mention in the *Bar Harbor Record* for July 30, 1891, pointed out what most people already knew: "Formerly access to the mountain could be obtained by means of the cog railroad, but it was not patronized sufficiently to warrant its continuance, and this year it has been abandoned."

On January 17, 1893, the Hancock County sheriff's department conducted a sale of GMR property at the law offices of Luere B. Deasy and John T. Higgins in Bar Harbor.[50] W. A. Milliken purchased the stern-wheeler *Wauwinet*. Daniel and Perry Brewer, together with Orient Carpenter, bought the summit hotel. The furniture and other fixtures went to J. McCarthy, formerly an engineer on the railway.[51] Local artist J. C. Manchester obtained one of the passenger cars and converted it into a Main Street studio for his paintings.[52] Later it served as a souvenir stand and a cobbler shop.[53] Liveryman William H. Puffer bought the other, and it became a stall on South Street, where he kept horses.[54] No one expressed an interest in either of the two locomotives, and they remained undisturbed at the base of the mountain.

The GMR Locomotives Live On

Little more than two years after the sale of GMR's assets, the defunct company's two locomotives experienced an unexpected rebirth of activity. On May 23, 1895, a devastating fire swept through many of the buildings at the Mount Washington Railway's base station at Marshfield, New Hampshire. Two of the railroad's

Following the demise of the Green Mountain Railway in 1890, company management was unable to dispose of the two locomotives, and they languished near the shore of Eagle Lake. In May 1895 a disastrous fire destroyed much of the Mount Washington Railway's rolling stock. One of the locomotives damaged beyond repair was *Cloud,* built in 1876 and shown here on Jacob's Ladder, a 300-foot trestle that attained the steepest pitch on the Mount Washington road—an amazing 37.41 degrees.

Mount Desert Island Historical Society, Mount Desert

Mount Washington Railway officials, desperate to replace fire-ravaged rolling stock in time for the 1895 season, purchased the two derelict Green Mountain Railway locomotives and had them transported to New Hampshire, where they began service that summer. Although extensively rebuilt over the years, both engines continue to serve at Mount Washington. GMR locomotive No. 1 now carries the name *Chocorua* (above), while No. 2 is known as *Agiocochook* (below).

Courtesy of Mount Washington Railway Company

seven locomotives were so badly damaged they had to be scrapped. Two others were salvageable, but required extensive, time-consuming rebuilding.[55] A pair of passenger cars, a baggage car, and a freight car were also destroyed.[56] The loss placed the railway's owners—since 1889, the Concord & Montreal Railroad Company (C&M)—in an uncomfortable predicament. With the summer season little more than a month away, the firm needed replacement locomotives in a hurry, if it were going to operate on a full schedule.

Word soon reached C&M that the two GMR locomotives were languishing at the foot of Green Mountain. Within ten days the company had purchased the idle "iron horses" and arranged to have them partially dismantled, to facilitate their shipment via the Maine Central Railroad from neighboring Mount Desert Ferry (Hancock Point) to Mount Washington.[57] Although extensively rebuilt over the years, to the extent that few, if any, original parts remain, the two former Green Mountain Railway locomotives are still operating on Mount Washington. No. 1 (*Mount Desert*) was renumbered "4" and now goes under the name *Chocorua*. No. 2 was first designated "5," renumbered "3" in 1934 and given the name *Base Station*, before being dubbed *Agiocochook* in 1995.[58]

CHAPTER SIX

Clergue Moves On

A Bevy of Bangor-Based Businesses

Seemingly unfazed by the setback to his vision of a street railway on Mount Desert Island, Frank Clergue kept busy seeking support for an ongoing string of investment firms he continued to devise. Corporation papers filed in Bangor as early as 1884 reveal he had developed plans for a series of speculative endeavors even before the MDI railroad scheme had stirred any organized opposition. In fact, during a nine-year span (1884–1893) Clergue and a variety of business partners— most notably, fellow attorneys Frederick Laughton and Melville H. Wardwell— teamed up to form as many as 20 companies. The proposed concerns involved such diverse activities as: hotel management, a steamship line, ice harvesting, land development and improvement, timber and wood products, water works, and hydroelectric power. Most were little more than paper corporations, without financial backing, although in 1888 Clergue did purchase the Veazie Lumber Company, including a saw mill, dam, and water rights, for $20,000.[1]

During the fall of 1888 Frank Clergue traveled to Russia and Persia (Iran), in an effort to convince Persian authorities to grant him permission to construct and operate a national railroad and an extensive system of public utilities. The deal reportedly fell through after the Russian government intervened and gained the first right-of-refusal on the projects. During the trip Clergue wrote several letters to his mother, including this, the first of four pages dated December 27. None of the correspondence provides details of the proposed business ventures.

Sault Ste. Marie (Ontario) Public Library

Fragmentary evidence suggests that during the late 1880s Frank Clergue also tried his hand at an unusually bold venture in southwest Asia. Ostensibly learning from contacts in London that the Persian government was eager to acquire railroads and public utilities, in September 1888 he established the Bangor-based Persia Company. The expressed purpose was the "carrying on all kinds of manufacturing and commercial businesses (and) undertaking the construction and carrying on of public works of every description" in Persia (now Iran). The following April he formed the Persia Petroleum Company and the City of Teheran Water Works[2] and announced he'd been granted approval to build a railroad across the middle-Eastern country. The venture presumably collapsed when the Russian government struck a deal with Muhammad Ali, Shah of Persia, for the first right-of-refusal in connection with any railroad construction in that country during the next five years.[3] Surviving letters dated December 1888 reveal that Clergue wrote to his mother in Bangor while he was enroute to Russia and during a stay in Teheran, although none contains specifics of actual business negotiations.[4]

Independent of his wide-ranging entrepreneurial dealings, Frank Clergue simultaneously pursued more conventional callings in Bangor. In 1887 he helped organize the Eastern Trust and Banking Company and became its first president.[5] He briefly served on the editorial staff at the *Bangor Daily Whig & Courier* and reported the 1888 trial of Charles Stain and Oliver Cromwell—brash, young bank robbers who were convicted of murdering Charles Barron, treasurer of the Dexter Savings Bank.[6]

Around 1891 Clergue again looked far afield in connection with another venturesome scheme, reportedly using English capital to set up a bank and finance a shipyard/drydock complex in Mobile, Alabama. As with nearly all his previous undertakings, the ambitious project failed.[7]

In 1894 Frank Clergue moved to Canada, settling in the then-remote village of Sault Ste. Marie, Ontario, where he undertook a grand plan to attract a wave of new industry to the surrounding area.

Sault Ste. Marie (Ontario) Public Library

Frank Clergue introduced hydroelectric power to Sault Ste. Marie, Ontario, in 1895 and rapidly transformed the once sleepy community into a bustling infrastructure of mutually dependent iron and nickel mines, pulp and paper mills, and interconnecting rail facilities. The Sault waterfront rapidly became the focal point for a beehive of passenger and freight arrivals and departures.

Sault Ste. Marie (Ontario) Public Library

An Epic Canadian Venture

Although Frank Clergue continued to reside in Bangor through 1893, by this time his primary business pursuits involved locations outside Maine. By 1894 he had allied himself with a group of Philadelphia-area capitalists looking for hydroelectric investment opportunities in such still-remote areas as east-central Canada. That September Clergue and Edwin Varian Douglas, one of the principal financiers, traveled to Sault Ste. Marie, Ontario. There they met with local officials and presented a multi-faceted plan to purchase the town's interest in a partially completed, but insolvent hydro project on the neighboring St. Mary's River. In early October Clergue and Douglas reached a two-part agreement with the Sault Ste. Marie Town Council, whereby they: (1) acquired the Ontario and Sault Ste. Marie Water, Light and Power Company, including an unfinished canal and related power plant; and (2) secured the exclusive right to supply water and power to the town.[8]

The comprehensive municipal pact became the starting point for Frank Clergue's sweeping efforts to utilize hydroelectricity to lure substantial new industry to the Sault Ste. Marie area. Renaming his new acquisition the Lake Superior Power Company, he set about getting it operating with quadruple the originally intended capacity. To help implement the process he purchased an operating power canal in neighboring Sault Ste. Marie, Michigan, and leased the Tagona Water and Power Company.[9]

Much to Clergue's chagrin the completed hydro plant failed to attract any business, and he realized he would have to create demand for the electricity by establishing his own commerce. With the further financial backing of his investors and a grant of two million acres of forest land from the Canadian government,

CASTALIA.
THE ... STEAMSHIP COMPANY.

Clergue (in 1896) launched the Sault Ste. Marie Pulp & Paper Company, to produce marketable commodities that would underwrite both the mill's startup costs and the power plant's recent construction.[10]

Ever the visionary, Clergue was not content with the completion of the pulp and paper mill. In fact, it was merely the first in a rapidly constructed network of related businesses he located at the Sault during the next few years. Initially he built a sulfite mill and acquired a nickel mine, to provide the chemicals for a more durable, cost-effective dry pulp product. Next came a ferro-nickel plant, to use the leftover nickel and iron following the extraction of the acid gas necessary for the chemical pulp. Before the end of the century he acquired and constructed a series of mines and plants, each mutually dependent on St. Mary's hydro power—and one another—for their individual success. Early on he launched a railroad to transport critical raw materials—particularly iron ore, nickel, and wood pulp—to supply the numerous industrial sites.[11] In 1897 he placed the entire network under an umbrella agency called the Consolidated Lake Superior Company (CLS).[12]

The Clergue Empire Collapses

To most, the spate of commercial activity in and around the Sault must have seemed a financial bonanza for Clergue and his partnership, but by early 1898 CLS began experiencing ominous signs of financial difficulty. To meet a commitment for a pending land purchase, the firm was forced to borrow $55,000 from the Provident Life and Trust Company of Philadelphia and $75,000 from the Imperial Bank of Canada. The two loans were merely the first in a series of similar emergency measures, as the growing fiscal demands of CLS' various enterprises increasingly outstripped any earnings they ultimately realized.[13]

In May 1901 CLS incorporated the Algoma Steel Company, the most ambitious undertaking to date. Financed principally by stock sales in Philadelphia and New York, the fledgling manufacturing, construction, and mining firm began producing steel in February 1902. After an early lot failed to meet industry standards, the company lost several essential contracts and in December had to temporarily shut down. Work resumed spasmodically the following year, although production never reached anticipated (or promised) levels, causing further disruptions and delays.[14] Algoma survived, principally by contracting with the Dominion Government to provide steel and pig iron, for which it collected lucrative provincial and federal bounties. During the four years between mid-1902 and mid-1906, the company received nearly one million dollars in preferential payments.

Clergue blamed Algoma's difficulty in obtaining additional contracts on Canadian ministry officials' failure to provide the country's emerging steel industry with tariffs against foreign competition. And while Parliament did pass protective legislation before the end of 1903, by then Algoma had again closed its doors. In fact, earlier in the year the company's investors had forced Clergue to resign his post as general manager at CLS, relegating him to an advisory capacity on the board of directors. And he lost that standing in 1908.

Although Algoma got past its early troubles and went on to become a major integrated steel giant, CLS went bankrupt in September 1903, with liabilities totaling more than eleven million dollars. Restructured in 1904, the old company was rechristened Lake Superior Corporation, under the leadership of C. D. Warren, and headquartered in New York.

Later Life Activities

Frank Clergue left Sault Ste. Marie in 1909 and moved to Montreal. Still the spirited promoter and salesman, he attempted to gain public support for a transcontinental railroad—the North Railway—across northern Canada, but an emerging economic downturn precluded any actual construction.

In 1915 Clergue traveled to Russia, where he negotiated a contract with the tsarist government for several million shrapnel and high-explosive shells manufactured by the Canadian Car and Foundry Company, a Montreal firm on whose board Clergue would sit (and be the principal stockholder) from 1920 until his death nearly twenty years later. In January 1917 many of the munitions were destroyed in a warehouse fire at Kingsland, New Jersey. During this period Clergue also served as president of the Universal Engineering Corporation, an enterprise he created, and the Connecticut-based Waterbury Tool Company, a firm acquired in 1935 by the newly formed Sperry Corporation.

Through the late 1920s and early 1930s, Frank Clergue used his still-compelling powers of persuasion to lobby (both in Ottawa and in Washington) for an improved St. Lawrence Seaway. Afterward he again went abroad, endeavoring to sell railroad rolling stock and related equipment to the Japanese-controlled puppet government in Manchuria.[15] In 1937 he returned one last time to Sault Ste. Marie, to attend a testimonial banquet held in his honor.[16]

Francis Hector Clergue died in Montreal on January 19, 1939, a few days after suffering a heart attack. He was 82 years old. His sister, Gertrude, who was living with him at the time of his death, continued to reside in the house they shared at 3522 Mountain Road.[17] He, his father, mother, two brothers, and a sister,

During his later life Frank Clergue lived in Montreal, Quebec, where he died in 1939, at the age of 82. He is buried at the Mount Hope Cemetery in Bangor, in an unassuming plot alongside several family members.

Author's Collection

are buried at Mount Hope Cemetery in Bangor, in a lot near the northern end of the burying ground that Frank had purchased in 1902.[18]

The Clergue Legacy

Frank Clergue left behind a distinctive legacy. His jaunty approach and aplomb, masterfully complemented by a persuasive and magnetic appeal, enabled him to

Francis H. Clergue is remembered in Canada as a visionary who initiated the country's first integrated industrial empire. In 1995 the Sault Ste. Marie (Ontario) Chamber of Commerce issued a two-dollar municipal trade token to celebrate his legacy and commemorate the centennial of the Sault Ste. Marie Canal, one of Clergue's first local undertakings.

Courtesy of Sault Ste. Marie (Ontario) Chamber of Commerce

convince all but the strongest doubters of the unquestionable merits of his many far-sighted schemes. On countless occasions he convinced potential investors to part with vast sums of money on ventures over which they would otherwise have remained strongly skeptical, if not totally unbelieving. And while he was undoubtedly sincere in his beliefs and utterly convinced he could bring them to pass, his "vision occasionally outran his judgment, and at times he took things for granted that had not been proven."[19]

Perhaps a victim of his own enthusiasm and verve, Frank Clergue typically plunged ahead with reckless abandon and fiscal irresponsibility, seemingly unaware (or ignorant) of the more immediate, often unfavorable consequences of his otherwise well-intended actions. Despite his ambitions and efforts, most of his endeavors failed completely, and those that survived did so only after his successors had labored mightily for protracted periods to untangle countless difficult situations.

Despite the shortcomings Clergue is remembered favorably today as a visionary at the Sault and widely regarded as the father of Canada's first integrated industrial empire. Descendant firms of his former holdings still prevail within the local economy, most notably Algoma Steel Inc., the St. Mary's Paper Company, and Great Lakes Power Ltd.

The Clergue name likewise remains much in evidence around Sault Ste. Marie. Since 1982 the Francis H. Clergue Generating Station, on the St. Mary's, has been a key element in Great Lakes Power's network of hydro stations supplying the area's industrial and residential power needs. Along the waterfront, 8.4-acre Clergue Park displays a bronze plaque, erected in 1948 by Canada's Historic Sites and Monuments Board, recognizing Francis Clergue as the individual responsible for the industrial development of Sault Ste. Marie. On Queen Street the Ermatinger/Clergue National Historic Site includes the early nineteenth century blockhouse where Clergue resided for a time. At the 1952 Francis H. Clergue Public School, on Weldon Street, upwards of 300 English-speaking children—senior kindergarten through grade three—receive special immersion in the French language. Intown, Clergue Street is one of the public thoroughfares intersecting Northern Avenue West.

In 1995 the Sault Ste. Marie Chamber of Commerce recognized Francis Clergue's contribution to the region by placing his countenance on a two-dollar municipal trade token, issued to commemorate the centennial of the opening of the Sault Ste. Marie Canal, which Clergue completed and established. The coin, struck in a variety of metals, was legal tender in the local community through September 30 that year.

EPILOGUE

After the Green Mountain Railway ceased running, the Summit House continued to operate for a few more years, but never on the scale or with the elegance it had previously. By the mid-1890s the entire operation had become dubious. Persistent rumors of illicit goings-on finally prompted authorities to investigate. On August 21, 1895, a county sheriff and three police officers raided the property, seized a large amount of liquor (in violation of Maine's prohibition law of 1846), and arrested proprietor J. M. McFarland and three young girls. Halfway down the mountain, McFarland jumped from the officers' buckboard and tried to escape into the nearby woods. He was recaptured after a short chase.[1] The Summit House never reopened.

Bound over to the October term of the Supreme Judicial Court in Ellsworth, McFarland pleaded guilty before presiding judge Andrew Wiswell and was sentenced to six months in jail.[2] McFarland's prior conduct had been less than honorable and perhaps contributed to the severity of the sentence. The previous month he had been arrested for assault in Bar Harbor. Previously, as road commissioner for the town of Eden, he was deposed at a special meeting for overdrawing his appropriated $3,000 without approval.[3]

In the wake of the incident the *Ellsworth American* published the following item:

> The raiding of the once-celebrated Green Mountain House recalls
> the early days of Bar Harbor's boom . . . The beautiful trip by buckboard
> to Eagle Lake, the sail across the lake to the foot of Green Mountain and

The Summit House atop Green Mountain continued to operate until 1895, but with dwindling success. The following summer much of the structure was dismantled and the remaining skeletal framework burned.

Mount Desert Island Historical Society, Mount Desert

a ride up the railway to the summit were features of the resort. Now all this is gone, and there remain but the dilapidated wreck of a pier, a few rickety buildings, rotting ties and rusty rails. How frail a thing is fame![4]

Marked by scandal the Summit House had become a black eye for MDI residents. During the summer of 1896 much of the once-imposing structure was taken down. The best timbers and boards were saved, leaving only a rickety shell which needed to be burned to be disposed of properly. Several people living in nearby Otter Creek objected to having the surviving framework set afire. They were afraid the surrounding woods might catch and a runaway blaze threaten their homes and community. The protest prompted the Bar Harbor Fire Department to assure those concerned that conditions would be suitable before they allowed anything on the mountain to be incinerated. The appropriate time arrived: the foggy, showery evening of September 19, when winds were essentially calm and the nearby woods wet. The Summit House's skeletal remains were ignited and quickly went up in smoke.[5]

By the end of 1896 most remaining traces of the Green Mountain Railway track had likewise been removed. In December the rails and assorted surplus iron were hauled to Nickerson & Spratt's Wharf in Bar Harbor, loaded aboard the schooner *Cambridge*, and taken to the Portland Rolling Mills, in South Portland, where they were recycled. The ties, stringers, and other wooden foundation pieces were left scattered along the roadway to rot.[6]

Over the next several years mixed vegetation encroached on the old roadbed, gradually obliterating its presence. In 1910 a nostalgic feature about the railroad appeared in the *Ellsworth American*, in which the writer commented how the route was still evident, but already "rather faint at times."[7] A dozen years later an item in the *Bar Harbor Times* mentioned that, "Not long ago it was possible . . . to trace the route of the old railroad up the slope of Green Mountain, but at the present time it is . . . hardly visible."[8]

At one point trailmakers marked the historic way with small stone cairns, and occasional ones are still evident along the stretch above the park loop road, north of Bubble Pond. Today the entire route is heavily overgrown, except where it crosses open ledges. In some places bushwhacking is the only way anyone

Several sections of the Green Mountain Railway track were laid directly on granite ledge, which eliminated the need for supporting trestlework. At one spot, roughly halfway up the mountain, crews constructed a 75-foot granite trestle to carry the rails across a small streambed. The side view (facing page) shows a closeup of some of the carefully set stones that remain solidly in place today. The uphill perspective (near left) is similar to ones the locomotive's engineer would have observed as he patiently drove the train toward the summit.

Author's Collection

Most of the surviving fixtures of the former Green Mountain Railway are iron anchor pins that held in place the foundation timbers supporting the track. They are most easily detected where parallel rows of the rusted shafts protrude from the exposed granite ledge over which the cog trains operated.

Author's Collection

A sole surviving section of **T**-rail alongside the Green Mountain Railway roadbed escaped work crews who tore up and removed the track in 1896.

attempting to trace the old line can faithfully follow the course. The best clues for identifying the exact location and direction are the surviving iron anchor pins that held the foundation logs in place. Most were never pulled from the ground, nor extracted from the ledges, and literally hundreds remain embedded where hardy crews first placed them.[9]

The passing of the Green Mountain Railway brought an end to a unique and colorful attempt to capitalize on Maine's budding resort business. Although doomed by a lack of sustainable interest, the curious attraction enabled thousands to marvel at the grandeurs of Mount Desert Island in a fashion most could have otherwise only imagined. It also brought the region a substantial measure of public awareness that has helped ensure its ongoing existence as a preeminent travel destination.

NOTES

INTRODUCTION

[1] Chapman, Carleton A. *The Geology of Acadia National Park*. Old Greenwich, Connecticut: The Chatham Press, 1962, 28–32.

[2] Sanger, David, and Prins, Harald E. L., *An Island in Time, Three Thousand Years of Cultural Exchange on Mount Desert Island*. Bar Harbor, Maine: The Robert Abbe Museum, Bulletin XII, 1994, 9–11.

[3] In 2004 the Royal Canadian Mint released a silver dollar collectors' coin and a 25-cent circulating coin to celebrate the Saint Croix Island settlement and observe the 400th anniversary of the first French settlement in North America. The reverse of both commemoratives depicts a likeness of the vessel that carried the colonists from Havre de Grace, France, to the New World.

[4] Champlain, Samuel de. *The voyages and explorations of Samuel de Champlain*. Vol. 1. New York: A. S. Barnes & Co., 1906, 83–84.

[5] Hale, Richard Walden, Jr. *The Story of Bar Harbor*. New York: Ives Washburn, Inc., 1949, 52–58.

[6] Ibid., 85–97.

[7] Hancock County Registry of Deeds, Ellsworth, Maine, Vol. 1, 518; Vol. 4, 74.

[8] Morison, Samuel Eliot. *The Story of Mount Desert Island Maine*. Boston: Little, Brown and Company, 1960, 27.

[9] Hale, 75–76, 99–100.

[10] Ibid., 126–131.

[11] Hill, Ruth Ann. *Discovering Old Bar Harbor and Acadia National Park*. Camden, Maine: Down East Books, 1996, 75–77.

[12] Hale, 154–155, 169–170.

CHAPTER ONE

[1] *The New Encyclopaedia Britannica*, 15th ed., s.v. "Rio de Janeiro."

[2] U.S. Department of Commerce. *United States Coast Pilot 1: Atlantic Coast, Eastport to Cape Cod*. Washington, D.C.: U.S. Government Printing Office, 1960, 70.

[3] Champlain, Samuel de, *The voyages and explorations of Samuel de Champlain*, Vol. 1. New York: A.S. Barnes & Co., 1906, 83–84.

[4] Morison, Samuel Eliot. "The Course of the *Arabella* from Cape Sable to Salem." Publications of The Colonial Society of Massachusetts, Vol. XXVII; Transactions 1927–1930: Boston, 1932, 285–295. Morison's study includes a copy of Winthrop's 1630 sketch, as well as a chart showing the *Arabella's* course across the Gulf of Maine. The essay contains a copy of a page from the 1729 edition of *The English Pilot, The Fourth Book*, entitled "The Making of the Land on the Coast of New England," which includes sketches of the "Mount Desart Hills."

[5] ———. *The Story of Mount Desert Island Maine*, 17.

[6] "A Plan of the Islands Eastward laying from Penobscot Bay & of the Granted Townships, with their Distances and Bearings from each Other and from the Continent, Agreable to a Resolve of the Great and General Court for the Province of the Massachusetts Bay—per John Jones & Barnabas Mason, Surveyors, February 13, 1765." Original ms. at the Massachusetts Archives, Boston, Massachusetts.

[7] Morison, *The Story of Mount Desert Island Maine*, 73. A photostat of Samuel Holland's "Chart of the Maine Coast, 1772" is in the William Otis Sawtelle Collections & Research Center, Park Headquarters, Acadia National Park, Bar Harbor, Maine.

[8] Des Barres, Joseph F. W. *Charts of the Coast and Harbors of New England . . .*, Vol. 3, *Atlantic Neptune*. London, 1780. An original is in the Osher Collection, Osher Map Library and Smith Center for Cartographic Education, University of Southern Maine, Portland, Maine. Original Samuel Holland copper engravings entitled "Penobscot Bay and Frenchman's Bay" (1776) and "The Coast of New England" (1781), both of which depict/identify Mount Desert Island, are at the Deer Isle Granite Museum, Stonington, Maine. A four-volume facsimile edition: *The Atlantic Neptune* (Barre, Massachusetts: Barre Publishing Co., 1966–1969) is part of the Special Collections at the Fogler Library, University of Maine, Orono, Maine.

[9] Peters, John & James. *Survey of the De Gregoire half of the Island, 1807*. Original ms. at the Bar Harbor Historical Society, Bar Harbor, Maine.

[10] Mazlish, Anne, ed. *The Tracy Log Book, 1855, A Month in Summer*. Bar Harbor, Maine: Acadia Publishing Company, 1997, 65.

[11] Walling, H. F. *Topographic Map of Hancock Co.* New York: Lee & Marsh, 1860.

[12] Martin, Clara Barnes. *Mount Desert on the Coast of Maine*. Portland, Maine: B. Thurston and Company, 1867, 6.

[13] DeCosta, Benjamin F. *Rambles in Mount Desert: with Sketches of Travel on the New-England Coast from Isles of Shoals to Grand Menan*. New York: A. D. F. Randall & Co.; Boston: A. Williams & Co., 1871, 83.

[14] *Bar Harbor Times*, February 11, 1931.

[15] Morison letter to Sen. Harold L. Ickes, May 27, 1933. Copy on file at U. S. Board on Geographic Names, Washington, D. C.

[16] Morison, *The Story of Mount Desert Island Maine*, 4–5.

[17] Sweetser, M. F. *Chisholm's Mount-Desert guide-book*. Portland, Maine: Chisholm Bros., [1888?].

[18] Hancock County Registry of Deeds, Vol. 81, 211; Vol. 82, 139; Vol. 106, 26; Vol. 131, 341.

[19] Dorr, George B. *The Story of Acadia National Park*. Bar Harbor, Maine: Acadia Publishing Co., 1985, 6–8; 35–45.

[20] Slotten, Hugh Richard. *Patronage, Practice, and the Culture of American Science: Alexander Dallas Bache and the U. S. Coast Survey*. Cambridge, England: Cambridge University Press, 1994, 61.

[21] "The Field Work." Undated e-document from the National Oceanic and Atmospheric Administration's Central Library, Washington, D. C., available from http://www.lib.noaa.gov/edocs/BACHE4.htm#NEWENGLAND; INTERNET.

[22] Hale, 129.

[23] *Report of the Superintendent of the United States Coast Survey, showing the Progress of the Survey during the Year 1853*, Sen. Exec. Doc. No. 14, 33rd Cong., 1st Sess., 192.

[24] *Report of the Superintendent of the United States Coast Survey, showing the Progress of the Survey during the Year 1855*, H. R. Exec. Doc. No. 6, 34th Cong., 1st Sess., 35.

[25] Hale, 128–129.

[26] *Ellsworth American*, August 17, 1866.

[27] DeCosta, 85–86.

[28] Hancock County Registry of Deeds, Vol. 131, 341.

[29] Hale, Jr., Richard Walden. "Cadillac's Old Green Mountain Railway." *Down East* 3 (July 1957), 42.

[30] DeCosta, 93.

[31] *Bangor Daily Whig & Courier*, March 31, 1883.

[32] *Mount Desert Herald*, August 8, 1884.

[33] Ibid., January 17, 1883.

[34] Ibid., August 6, 1881.

[35] Ibid., August 4, 1882.

[36] Ibid., August 19, 1882.

CHAPTER TWO

[1] "Francis H. Clergue: the Personality." Undated biographical sketch in the collections of the Sault Ste. Marie (Ontario) Public Library, available from collections.ic.gc.ca/ssm/pages/english/clergue2.html; INTERNET.

[2] Records of the Mount Hope Cemetery, Bangor, Maine.

[3] Bangor, City of. *Annual Reports . . . for the Municipal Year 1884–85*. Bangor: B. A. Burr, Whig & Courier Job Print., 1885.

[4] Clergue T. Jones (great nephew of Francis H. Clergue), conversation with author, Ellsworth, Maine, June 5, 2003.

[5] *Thomas Edison and the Electric Railroad*. Undated article available from www.edisonnj.org; INTERNET.

[6] *Legacies: Frank J. Sprague (1857–1934)*. Undated broadside published by the IEEE (Institute of Electrical and Electronics Engineers) History Center, Rutgers University, New Brunswick, New Jersey.

[7] McDowall, Duncan. *Steel at the Sault: Francis H. Clergue, Sir James Dunn, and the Algoma Steel Corporation 1901–1956.* University of Toronto Press: Toronto, Buffalo, London, 1984, 28.

[8] *Mount Desert Herald,* January 4, 1883.

[9] *Green Mountain Railway Certificate of Corporation, November 23, 1882,* Records of the Maine Secretary of State, reposited at the Maine State Archives, Augusta, Maine.

[10] Joslin, Richard S., *Sylvester Marsh and the Cog Railway,* (Privately printed, 2000), 1–4.

[11] Ibid., 5–6.

[12] Ibid., 8–14.

[13] Ibid., 15, 27, 38.

[14] Hancock County Registry of Deeds, Vol. 189, 139–140, 145.

[15] *Bangor Commercial,* January 11, 1883.

[16] *Bangor Daily Whig & Courier,* May 31, 1883.

[17] *Eastern Argus,* June 26, 1883.

[18] *Bangor Daily Whig & Courier,* March 1, 1883.

[19] Public Laws of Maine: 1876, Chapter 120, 85.

[20] *Green Mountain Railway Articles of Association,* Records of the Secretary of State: 1883, Vol. 5, 397, reposited at the Maine State Archives, Augusta, Maine.

[21] Public and Special Laws of Maine: 1883, Chapter 181, 244.

[22] *Eastern Argus,* June 26, 1883.

[23] *Bangor Commercial,* February 5 & 21 1883.

CHAPTER THREE

[1] *Mount Desert Herald*, February 11, 1883.

[2] Ibid., May 10, 1883.

[3] Ibid., April 19, 1883.

[4] Ibid., March 1, 1883.

[5] Ibid., April 19, 1883.

[6] *Bangor Daily Whig & Courier*, May 12, 1883.

[7] The author examined the site during a hike along the former Green Mountain Railway roadbed, July 6, 2001.

[8] *Mount Desert Herald*, May 10, 1883.

[9] *Ellsworth American*, April 5, 1883.

[10] *Mount Desert Herald*, March 1, 1883.

[11] *Eastern Argus*, June 26, 1883.

[12] *Mount Desert Herald*, April 12, 1883.

[13] *Bangor Daily Whig & Courier*, May 12, 1883.

[14] *Mount Desert Herald*, June 7, 1883.

[15] *Eastern Argus*, June 26, 1883.

[16] *Bangor Daily Whig & Courier*, March 1, 1883.

[17] *Mount Desert Herald*, April 19, 1883.

[18] *Eastern Argus*, April 26, 1883.

[19] *Bangor Daily Whig & Courier*, May 12, 1883.

[20] *Mount Desert Herald*, May 10, 1883.

[21] *Bangor Daily Whig & Courier*, May 12, 1883.

[22] Joslin, 25.

[23] *Mount Desert Herald*, May 3, 1883.

[24] *Mount Desert Herald*, April 12, 1883.

[25] *Bangor Daily Whig & Courier*, May 12, 1883.

[26] Bradlee, Francis B. C. *Some Account of Steam Navigation in New England*. Salem, Massachusetts: The Essex Institute, 1920, 30.

[27] *Mount Desert Herald*, April 19, 1883.

[28] Ibid., May 3, 1883.

[29] Ibid., May 10, 1883.

[30] *Bangor Daily Whig & Courier*, May 31, 1883.

[31] Ibid., June 20, 1883.

[32] *Mount Desert Herald*, March 8, 1883.

[33] *Bangor Daily Whig & Courier*, March 31, 1883.

[34] Ibid., April 23, 1883.

[35] Ibid., May 12, 1883.

[36] *Eastern Argus*, June 26, 1883.

[37] *Boston Post*, June 26, 1883.

[38] *Mount Desert Herald*, July 12, 1883.

[39] Ibid., August 23, 1883.

[40] *The Journals of John Edward Godfrey, Bangor, Maine*, Vol. 3, 1878–1884. Rockland, Maine: Courier-Gazette, 1985, 298.

[41] *Mount Desert Herald*, September 13, 1883.

[42] Ibid., September 6, 1883.

[43] Ibid., September 20, 1883.

[44] *1884 Annual Report of the Maine Board of Railroad Commissioners*, unpaged tabular appendix.

[45] *Mount Desert Herald*, October 25, 1883.

[46] Ibid., November 1, 1883.

CHAPTER FOUR

[1] *Mount Desert Herald*, November 1, 1883–February 7, 1884.

[2] Ibid., August 22, 1884.

[3] Ibid., June 28, 1889.

CHAPTER FIVE

[1] *Mount Desert Herald*, May 8, 1884.

[2] Ibid., June 26, 1884.

[3] *1884 Annual Report of the Maine Board of Railroad Commissioners*, 17.

[4] *Mount Desert Herald*, June 19, 1884.

[5] Ibid., August 8, 1884.

[6] Guth, Edith B. "I Remember . . . The Green Mountain Fire." *Down East*, 13 (July 1967), 71.

[7] *Mount Desert Herald*, August 8, 1884.

[8] Ibid., September 5, 1884.

[9] Ibid., September 26, 1884.

[10] Ibid., October 3, 1884.

[11] Ibid., March 27, 1885.

[12] Ibid., May 22, 1885.

[13] *Mount Desert Herald*, June 26, 1885.

[14] Ibid., May 14, 1886.

[15] *Bar Harbor Record*, August 1, 1889.

[16] *1889 Annual Report of the Maine Board of Railroad Commissioners*, 32.

[17] *Mount Desert Herald*, October 1, 1886.

[18] Ibid., July 16, 1886.

[19] *The Daily Herald*, July 13, 1886.

[20] *1887 Annual Report of the Maine Board of Railroad Commissioners*, 26. The annual financial abstract submitted by the Green Mountain Railway to the Maine Board of Railroad Commissioners does not include the number of passengers carried on the company's trains during the line's 1887 operating season. The estimated figure used here is based on a comparison of the ratios of GMR's passengers carried to net income during other years annual totals are available.

[21] *1888 Annual Report of the Maine Board of Railroad Commissioners*, 66.

[22] *1889 Annual Report of the Maine Board of Railroad Commissioners*, 83.

[23] These include: Hale, *The Story of Bar Harbor*, 160; Matter, Frank "The Infamous Green Mountain Railway." *Acadia Weekly* Vol. X, no. 18 (October 5–11, 1997), 7–9, 12; Burt, Frank H. "Mount Desert's Mountain Railway." *Appalachia* Vol. IX, No. 12, (December 1943), 435–440.

[24] *Mount Desert Herald*, June 21, 1883.

[25] Ibid., August 6, 1881.

[26] Ibid., July 27, 1888.

[27] *Bar Harbor Record*, August 23, 1888.

[28] *Mount Desert Herald*, August 3, 1888.

[29] *Bar Harbor Record*, August 2, 1888.

[30] Ibid., October 25, 1888.

[31] *Mount Desert Herald*, June 14, 1889.

[32] Ibid., July 12, 1889.

[33] *Bar Harbor Record*, July 25, 1889.

[34] Ibid., August 1, 1889.

[35] Ibid., August 8, 1889.

[36] Ibid., July 25, 1889.

[37] *Bangor Commercial*, February 24, 1883.

[38] *Evolution of the Signal Service Years (1600–1891)*, undated (NOAA history) article available from www.history.noaa.gov/stories/evolut.html; INTERNET.

[39] *Bar Harbor Record*, October 18, 1888.

[40] *Mount Desert Herald*, March 8, 1889.

[41] Ibid., May 23, 1889.

[42] Ibid., July 4, 1889.

[43] Ibid., September 19, 1889.

[44] Ibid., May 29, 1890.

[45] National Archives, Records Describing Weather Stations, 1883–1904 ("Miscellaneous Books"), Vol 10, 166–167, Green Mt., Maine. RG 27.

[46] *Bar Harbor Record*, May 1, 1890.

[47] Ibid., September 4, 1890.

[48] *Mount Desert Herald*, September 19, 1890.

[49] *1890 Annual Report of the Maine Board of Railroad Commissioners*, 81.

[50] *Bar Harbor Record*, January 19, 1893.

[51] *Eastern Argus*, February 2, 1893.

[52] *Bar Harbor Record*, March 31, 1897.

[53] *Bangor Daily News*, February 7, 1916.

[54] *Bar Harbor Record*, March 18, 1896.

[55] *Bangor Daily Whig & Courier*, May 24, 1895.

[56] *Among The Clouds*, July 13, 1895.

[57] *Bangor Courier*, June 4, 1895.

[58] "Current Roster of Locomotives" available from www.cog-railway.com/alltime.html; INTERNET.

CHAPTER SIX

[1] *Certificates of Organizations of Corporations,* Vol. 1, 196–413, Penobscot County Registry of Deeds, Bangor, Maine.

[2] Ibid., Vol. 1, 266.

[3] Eldon, Donald. "The Career of Francis H. Clergue," *Explorations in Entrepreneurial History* (April 1951), 254–263.

[4] Letters from F. H. Clergue to family members during a trip to Russia and Persia: December 1888–January 1889. File 14, Box 30, Clergue Family Papers, collections of the Sault Ste. Marie (Ontario) Public Library.

[5] *Bangor Daily Commercial,* February 27, 1937.

[6] *Bangor Daily News,* August 21, 1937.

[7] McDowall, 29.

[8] *The Arrival of Francis H. Clergue,* undated article available from www.city.sault-ste-marie.on.ca/library/clergue/arrival.htm; INTERNET.

[9] *Lake Superior Power Company Limited,* undated article available from www.soonet.ca/publibrary/pages/lake.htm; INTERNET.

[10] *A History of the Events Surrounding Edison Sault Electric Company,* undated article available from www.edisonsault.com/100years/history.htm; INTERNET.

[11] *The Industrialization Process,* undated article available from www.city.sault-ste-marie.on.ca/library/clergue/industri.htm; INTERNET.

[12] McDowall, 30.

[13] *Lake Superior Power Company Limited,* undated article available from www.soonet.ca/publibrary/pages/lake.htm; INTERNET

[14] *The Algoma Steel Company Limited*, undated article available from www.soonet.ca/publibrary/pages/steel.htm; INTERNET

[15] McDowall, 34–35, 45–48.

[16] *Sault Daily Star*, February 16, 1937.

[17] *Bangor Daily Commercial*, January 20, 1939.

[18] Records of the Mount Hope Cemetery, Bangor, Maine.

[19] Gibson, T. W. *Mining in Ontario*. Toronto, 1937, 126–127.

EPILOGUE

[1] *Ellsworth American*, August 29, 1895.

[2] Ibid., October 17, 1895.

[3] *Bangor Daily Whig & Courier*, July 15, 1895.

[4] *Ellsworth American*, August 29, 1895.

[5] *Bar Harbor Record*, September 23, 1896.

[6] Ibid., December 30, 1896.

[7] *Ellsworth American*, September 21, 1910.

[8] *Bar Harbor Times*, September 13, 1922.

[9] In July 2001 and May 2002, the author hiked the entire length of the former Green Mountain Railway roadbed.

SELECT BIBLIOGRAPHY

Books, Articles, Papers

Bacon, George F. *Bangor: Its Points of Interest and its Representative Business Men; Including an Historical Sketch of Brewer.* Newark, N.J.: Glenwood Publishing Co., 1891.

Bangor, City of. *Annual Reports . . . for the Municipal Year 1884–85.* Bangor: B.A. Burr, Whig & Courier Job Print., 1885.

Bangor, Maine. *City Councils and Mayors, from Incorporation of the City, in 1834 to 1881 . . .* Bangor, Maine: B.A. Burr, 1881.

Bar Harbor Blue Book and Mount Desert Guide with Maps and Tables. Boston: Albert W. Bee, 1881.

Beeks, Dale R. "The Heliotrope." *Backsights*, Vol 11, No. 2 (July 1992), 14.

Belanger, Pamela A. *Inventing Acadia: Artists and Tourists at Mount Desert.* Rockland, Maine: The Farnsworth Art Museum, 1999.

Blanding, Edward M. "Bangor, Maine." *National Magazine*, 17 (1902–1903).

_____, comp. *The City of Bangor; the Industries, Resources, Attractions and Business Life of Bangor and its Environs.* Bangor, Maine: Industrial Journal, 1899.

Bradlee, Francis B.C. *Some Account of Steam Navigation in New England.* Salem, Massachusetts: The Essex Institute, 1920.

Bowen, Louise de Koven. *Baymeath.* Privately printed, 1944.

Buettell, Roger B. "The Bar Harbor Express." *Yankee* 31 (August 1967), 138–147.

Cameron, Mable Ward, *The Biographical Cyclopedia of American Women*, Vol. I. New York: Halvord Publishing Co., 1924.

Champlain, Samuel de. *The voyages and explorations of Samuel de Champlain*, Vol. 1. New York: A. S. Barnes & Co., 1906.

Chapman, Carleton A. *The Geology of Acadia National Park*. Old Greenwich, Connecticut: The Chatham Press, 1962.

Clergue, Francis H. *Address by Francis Clergue at a banquet given in his honor by the citizens of Sault Ste. Marie, Ont., Friday evening, February fifteenth, nineteen hundred and one*. Sault Ste. Marie, Ontario: Soo News Press, 1901.

_____. *An instance of industrial evolution in northern Ontario, Dominion of Canada: an address by Francis H. Clergue, Esq., president and manager of the Sault Ste. Marie Pulp & Paper Co., Sault Ste. Marie, Ont., delivered at a general meeting of the Board of Trade of the City of Toronto*. Toronto, 1900.

Francis H. Clergue, letters to family members written during a trip to Russia and Persia, December 1888–January 1889. File 14, Box 30, Clergue Family Papers, collections of the Sault Ste. Marie (Ontario) Public Library.

Colby's Atlas of the State of Maine, including statistics and descriptions of its history, educational system, geology, railroads, natural resources, summer resorts, and manufacturing interests, 3rd ed. Houlton, Maine: Colby & Stuart, 1887.

Cook, David S. *Above the Gravel Bar: Indian Canoe Routes In Maine*. Milo, Maine: Milo Printing Co., 1985.

DeCosta, B. F. *Rambles in Mount Desert: with Sketches of Travel on the New-England Coast from Isles of Shoals to Grand Menan*. New York: A. D. F. Randolph & Co.; Boston: A. Williams & Co., 1871.

Des Barres, Joseph F. W., *The Atlantic Neptune*, 4 vols. Barre, Massachusetts: Barre Publishing Co., 1966–1969.

Dodge, E. H. *Dodge's Guide Book to and over Mount Desert Island*. Portland, Maine: Loring, Short & Harmon, 1872.

Dorr, George B. *The Story of Acadia National Park*. Bar Harbor, Maine: Acadia Publishing Co., 1985.

Eldon, Donald. "The Entrepreneurial Career of F. H. Clergue." *Explorations in Entrepreneurial History* (April 1951), 254–268.

Epp, Ronald. Ph.D. "Acadia's Founder." *Friends of Acadia Journal*, Vol. 6, No. 2 (Summer 2001), 9–10.

____. "From Monument to Park: Voices of the Advocates." *Friends of Acadia Journal*, Vol. 7. No. 3 (Winter 2002–2003), 8–9.

Erikson, Dorothy Brewer. *Descendants of Thomas Brewer, Connecticut to Maine, 1682–1996, with allied families*. Boston, N. E. Historic Genealogical Society, 1996.

Fraser, Richard & Nancy. *A History of Maine Built Automobiles 1834–1934*. Privately printed, 1991.

Gibson, T. W. *Mining in Ontario*. Toronto, 1937, 126–127.

Godfrey, George Frederick. *A Sketch of Bangor*. Boston: James R. Osgood and Co., 1882.

Godfrey, John E. *History of Penobscot County, Maine, with Illustrations and Biographical Sketches*. Cleveland: Williams, Chase, 1882.

Green Mountain Railway and Cadillac Mountain files, William Otis Sawtelle Collections and Research Center, Acadia National Park headquarters, Bar Harbor, Maine.

Green Mountain Railway Articles of Association, Records of the Secretary of State: 1883, Vol. 5, 397, reposited at the Maine State Archives, Augusta, Maine.

Guth, Edith B. "I Remember . . . The Green Mountain Fire." *Down East*, 13 (July 1967), 71.

Hale, Richard Walden, Jr. "Cadillac's Old Green Mountain Railway." *Down East* 3 (July 1957), 40–43.

_____. *The Story of Bar Harbor*. Ives Washburn, Inc.: New York, 1949.

Hancock County (Maine), 1860: Library of Congress G&M land ownership map on microfiche. Washington, D. C.: Library of Congress G&M Division, 1983. Authors: H. F. Walling, Lee & Marsh, and Library of Congress/Geography and Map Division. PC 4354, Microfiche 583, No. 268. Originally published New York: Lee & Marsh, 1860.

Hancock County Registry of Deeds, *Index of Deeds*, Vols. 1, 4, 7, 58, 80–83, 103, 105–106, 130–131, 134, 182, 189, 193–194, 199–202, 223, 226, 231, 455. Ellsworth, Maine.

Heseltine, Charles D. "Bangor Street Railway." Transportation Bulletin No. 81, National Railway Historical Society, Inc. (Jan–Dec 1974), 5–11.

Hill, Ruth Ann. *Discovering Old Bar Harbor and Acadia National Park*. Camden, Maine: Down East Books, 1996.

Joslin, Richard S., *Sylvester Marsh and the Cog Railway*. Privately printed, 2000.

Joy, Barbara Ellen. *Historical Notes on Mount Desert Island*, Vols. I–III. Privately printed, 1966, 1974–1975.

Kidder, Glen M. *Railway to the Moon*. Littleton, New Hampshire: Privately printed, 1969.

Knowles' Bangor Business Almanac for 1875, with Historical Sketches of Bangor and its Business Enterprises. Charles Phelps Roberts, ed. Philadelphia: Dorrance, 1974.

Lapham, William Berry. *Bar Harbor and Mount Desert Island.* New York: Press of Liberty Printing Co., 1886.

"Lawyers Admitted to Practice in Courts of Penobscot County." *Bangor Historical Magazine*, 3 (1887–1888), 228–229.

Maine Public and Special Laws: 1883, Chapter 181, 244.

Maine Public Laws: 1876, Chapter 120, 85.

Maine, State of. *Annual Reports of the Maine Board of Railroad Commissioners*, Augusta, Maine, 1883–1890.

Martin, Clara Barnes. *Mount Desert, on the Coast of Maine.* Portland, Maine: B. Thurston and Company, 1867; 5th ed., Portland, Maine: Loring, Short & Harmon, 1880.

Mazlish, Anne, ed. *The Tracy Log Book, 1855, A Month in Summer.* Bar Harbor, Maine: Acadia Publishing Company, 1997.

McDowall, Duncan. *Steel at the Sault: Francis H. Clergue, Sir James Dunn, and the Algoma Steel Corporation 1901–1956.* University of Toronto Press: Toronto, Buffalo, London, 1984.

McFarlane, Arthur E. "Mr. Clergue of 'New Ontario.'" *The Saturday Evening Post*, Vol. 175, No. 11 (September 13, 1902), 3–4.

Morison, Samuel Eliot. *The Story of Mount Desert Island.* Boston: Little, Brown & Co., 1960.

Peirce Family Papers. Special Collections, Raymond H. Fogler Library, University of Maine at Orono.

Penobscot County Registry of Deeds, *Certificates of Organizations of Corporations*, Vol. 1, Bangor, Maine.

Peters, John and James. *Survey of the De Gregoire half of the Island, 1807.*

Rand, Edward Lothrop. *Flora of Mount Desert Island, Maine. A preliminary catalogue of the plants growing on Mount Desert and the adjacent islands.* Cambridge, Mass: J. Wilson and Son, 1894.

Roberts, Ann Rockefeller. *Mr. Rockefeller's Roads.* Camden, Maine: Down East Books, 1990.

Sanger, David, and Prins, Harald E. L., *An Island in Time, Three Thousand Years of Cultural Exchange on Mount Desert Island.* Bar Harbor, Maine: The Robert Abbe Museum, Bulletin XII, 1994.

Savage, Richard A. "The Bar Harbor Auto War." *Down East* 22 (August 1975), 66–69, 84, 87.

Slotten, Hugh Richard. *Patronage, Practice, and the Culture of American Science: Alexander Bache and the U. S. Coast Survey.* Cambridge, England: Cambridge University Press, 1994.

Street, George E. *Mount Desert: A History.* Edited by Samuel A. Eliot. 2nd rev. ed., Boston and New York: Houghton Mifflin Co., 1926.

Sweetser, M. F. *Chisholm's Mount-Desert guide-book.* Portland, Maine: Chisholm Bros., [1888?].

U. S. Department of Commerce. *United States Coast Pilot 1: Atlantic Coast, Eastport to Cape Cod.* Washington, D. C.: U. S. Government Printing Office, 1960.

Newspapers

Among The Clouds (Mount Washington, N. H.), July 13, 1895.

Bangor (Maine) *Daily Commercial*, January 11, 1883; February 5, 1883; February 27, 1937; January 20–21, 1939.

Bangor (Maine) *Daily News*, September 29, 1903; February 7, 1916; July 26, 1932; August 21, 1937; January 20, 1939.

Bangor (Maine) *Daily Whig & Courier*, March 31, 1883–June 20, 1883; June 4, 1895.

Bar Harbor (Maine) *Record*, August 2, 1888–December 30, 1896.

Bar Harbor (Maine) *Times*, September 13, 1922; February 11, 1931.

Boston Post, June 26, 1883.

Boston Sunday Herald, December 13, 1964.

Eastern Argus (Portland, Maine), April 26, 1883; June 26, 1883.

Ellsworth (Maine) *American*, August 17, 1866; April 5, 1883; October 17, 1895; September 21, 1910.

Montreal Gazette, January 20, 1939.

Montreal Daily Star, January 20, 1939.

Mount Desert Herald (Bar Harbor, Maine), August 6, 1881–September 19, 1890.

Sault Daily Star (Sault Ste. Marie, Ontario), February 16, 1937.

INDEX